Excel 2
Foundation to Expert Guide

Chris Voyse and Patrice Muse

Published by
Voyse Recognition Limited

September 2007

Voyse Recognition Limited • Century Business Centre • Manvers Way • Manvers
Rotherham • South Yorkshire • S63 5DA • 01709 300188
www.smart-pc-guides.com

© 2007 Voyse Recognition Limited

First Published in Great Britain in 2007

Voyse Recognition Limited
Century Business Centre
Manvers Way
Manvers
Rotherham
South Yorkshire
S63 5DA
01709 300188

ISBN 978-1-905657-23-0

Section 1: Foundation Level Objectives

- Introduction to Excel
- Creating New Worksheets
- Inputting Information into a Cell
- Opening and Saving Workbooks
- Introduction to Custom Lists
- Working with Simple Formula
- Relative and Absolute Formula
- Formatting Options
- Inserting Header and Footer
- Print Preview and Printing Options
- Creating a Simple Chart

Section 2: Intermediate Level Objectives

- Naming a Worksheet and Navigation
- Analysing Information in Different Worksheets
- Working with Multiple Sheets
- Generate 3-D Formula
- Freezing Panes and Split Windows
- Saving Workbooks in Different Formats
- Working with Different Charts
- Review of BODMAS
- Vertical and Horizontal Lookup Functions
- Inserting Comments
- Password Protection
- Filtering Data

Section 3: Expert Level Objectives

- Creating Range Names
- Auditing a Worksheet
- Using Watch Window
- Strings and Text Functions
- Logical Functions
- Outlining a Worksheet
- Data Consolidation
- Templates
- Scenario Manager
- Custom Views
- PivotTables
- Macros
- Quick Access Toolbar
- Excel File Formats
- Shortcut Keys

Table of Contents

Section 1: Foundation Level Objectives

- Introduction to Excel

- Creating New Worksheets

- Inputting Information into a Cell

- Opening and Saving Workbooks

- Introduction to Custom Lists

- Working with Simple Formula

- Relative and Absolute Formula

- Formatting Options

- Inserting Header and Footer

- Print Preview and Printing Options

- Creating a Simple Chart

Note: If you are working in Windows XP instead of Windows Vista, dialog boxes may look different but function in a similar way

Introducing the Excel Screen

Excel 2007 is a simple and efficient spreadsheet application released by Microsoft that runs in a Windows environment allowing the user to create and edit both small and large workbooks. It is user-friendly and easy to work with providing prompts to help the user identify icons on the screen that the user maybe unfamiliar with and takes the user through the various functions within this application.

Tour of the Screen

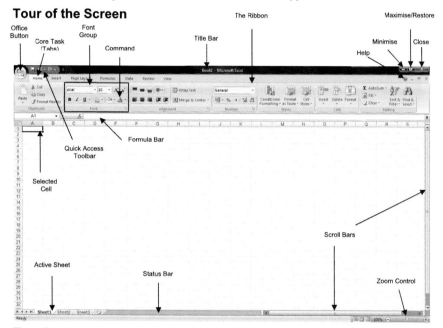

Figure 1

Office Button

In Excel 2007 the Office Button replaces the file menu found in previous versions of Excel and displays the commands for New, Open, Save, Print, Prepare, Send, Publish, Business Contact Manager and Close and the related options available under each command.

Title Bar

The Title Bar is highlighted in blue at the top of the screen and defines the programme that the user is in and the name of the Excel Workbook that the user has open. MS Excel will automatically display the default name, for example Book 1, in the Title Bar. Once the workbook has been saved, the saved name will be displayed in the Title Bar.

The Ribbon

The Ribbon is new to Excel 2007 and is the control centre to quickly help the user find the commands that help the user complete a task. The Ribbon is organised into three parts

1. **Core Tasks:** consisting of seven Tabs

   Home, Insert, Page Layout, Formulas, Data, Review and View

2. **Groups:** related items grouped together

3. **Commands:** buttons, boxes and menus that give instruction

The Ribbon organises the commands into logical groups all collected together under the Tabs with each Tab relating to a type of activity. Some Tabs only appear when they are needed whilst others are visible all the time.

To minimise the Ribbon double click with the left button on the active Tab, for example Home, the Ribbon and its commands disappear. Alternatively Ctrl F1 minimises the ribbon. To display the Ribbon and its commands, click with the left button on the any one of the Tabs.

Help

The Help icon can be found on the right hand side of the Ribbon.

Formula Bar

The Formula Bar is used for creating formula and displays the active cell.

Scroll Bars

Horizontal and Vertical scroll bars enable users to move around the workbook.

Sheet Tab

The Sheet Tab Sheet1 Sheet2 Sheet3 displays in white the active worksheet.

Page Layout View

Page Layout View is new to Excel 2007 making it easy to add headers and footers as well as adjust and turn margins on and off. Page Layout View enables the user to view the document as it will appear on a printed page. To activate Page Layout View:

1. Click the View Tab, select Page Layout View

2. Using the keyboard shortcuts press Alt W P

3. Alternatively select the Page Layout View icon in the Status Bar

Status Bar

The Status Bar is found at the bottom of the worksheet window and can be customised to display the features that the user wants to see. To customise the Status Bar

1. Press the right 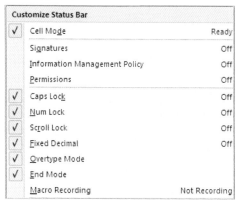 button on the Status Bar, the Customise Status Bar menu appears

Figure 2

2. To activate the Caps Lock so it is displayed in the Status Bar when in use

3. Click with the left ⌖ button on ▢ Caps Lock

4. A tick ▢ is displayed to indicate the feature has been activated

5. Click back in the worksheet

6. Press the ▢Caps key on the keyboard

7. ▢ Caps Lock is displayed in the Status Bar to show that it is activated

8. Click the ▢Caps key on the keyboard a second time to switch the feature off

Quick Access Toolbar

The Quick Access Toolbar can be found in the top section of the screen. It allows the user to display commands that are regularly used and that are independent of their associated Tabs. There is the option to locate the Quick Access Toolbar in two locations near to the top section of the screen.

Zoom Control

To use the Zoom Control drag with the left ⌖ button to increase (magnify) or decrease the worksheet to display the information larger or smaller on screen.

Opening Microsoft Excel

To open the Excel 2007 application, select the Start Button 🔵 , move the mouse

pointer ⃕ and pause over ▶ **All Programs** , click with the left

🖰 button on 🗀 Microsoft Office ; select 🅇 Microsoft Office Excel 2007 ,

click with the left 🖰 button to open the programme.

Creating a Shortcut to the Desktop

Creating a shortcut to the desktop enables quick access to an application, folder or
file, for example the Excel 2007 application. The shortcut can be identified by the
arrow 🡕 on the icon.

1. Move the mouse pointer ⃕ over   🅇 Microsoft Office Excel 2007

2. Click with the right 🖰 button, select   Send To   ▶

3. Choose 🖥 Desktop (create shortcut)

4. The Shortcut Key appears on the desktop 🗔

Understanding Worksheets

Each new workbook contains three worksheets, if more worksheets are required

1. Click on the Office Button 🔵 , select 📄 Excel Options

2. The Excel Options dialog appears

When creating new workbooks		
Use this font:	Arial	⌄
Font size:	10 ⌄	
Default view for new sheets:	Normal View ⌄	
Include this many sheets:	2 ⌃⌄	

Figure 3

3. Choose the option - When creating new workbooks

4. Select - Include this many **s**heets

5. Type in the number of sheets required or use the arrow keys

6. Press `OK` to set the new default number of worksheets

7. Click on the Office Button, select `New`

8. Choose `Create`, the new default worksheets appear

Moving Around Within a Worksheet

Excel references by a column reference and then a row reference. There are 16,384 columns and 1,048,576 rows in a worksheet.

1. Click in cell A1

2. Both the column and row references are highlighted in orange

Figure 4

3. The Formula Bar above column A displays the cell **A1**

4. When you select a cell a white cross ⊕ appears

5. To select a cell, click with the left button

6. There are a number of ways to move to a different cell

7. Use the arrow keys on the keyboard ↓ ↑ ← →

8. This will highlight the next cell reference

9. The cell reference is displayed in the Formula Bar

10. Alternatively press the `Tab` key, the new active cell is displayed

11. To move back a cell, hold down `Shift`, press the `Tab` key

12. Click on cell A1 using the left button

13. Hold down `Ctrl`, press → to display the final column in the worksheet

14. To return to column A1 hold down `Ctrl`, press ←

15. In cell A1 hold the `Ctrl` key down and select ↓

16. To return to Cell A1 hold the `Ctrl` key down and select ↑

Inserting Information into a Cell

1. When the mouse pointer ⩗ is moved in a cell a white cross appears ⬦
2. Move the mouse pointer ⩗ over cell G2
3. Click with the left 🖱 button to select cell G2
4. Type out the word January
5. As text is typed the information appears in the Formula Bar and the cell

Figure 5

6. To accept the information in G2 click on the blue tick ✓
7. Alternatively, press the Enter key on the keyboard
8. Text entered into a cell automatically aligns to the left January

Editing Information in a Cell

Excel 2007 allows the user to change information in several different ways. To go back a character, use the backspace key ⬅ on the keyboard.

1. Select the cell to be edited
2. Press F2, a flashing cursor appears to edit the cell contents as necessary
3. Alternatively, move the mouse over the cell you want to edit
4. As you move over the cell a white cross appears ⬦
5. Guide the white cross over the cell to be edited
6. Double click with the left 🖱 button
7. A flashing cursor appears where the cross was guided to appear
8. Edit the cell contents as necessary

Editing Information using the Formula Bar

1. Select the cell you want to edit
2. Move the left 🖱 button into the Formula Bar
3. Click with the left 🖱 button where the flashing cursor is to appear

Figure 6

4. Once edited click on the blue tick ✓ or press the Enter key

Exercise 1: - Creating and Saving a Worksheet

	A	B	C
1	Monthly Household Expenses		
2	Mortgage		£259.00
3	Rates		£27.00
4	Electricity		£13.00
5	Gas		£7.99
6	Television		£16.99
7	Telephone		£15.00
8	Insurance		£8.50
9	Food		£120.00
10			
11	Total		£467.48

1. Open a new workbook by clicking on the Office Button

2. Select the New Document icon [New], choose Blank Workbook [ ], click [Create], type the text shown in Exercise 1 above

3. Click on the [Home] Tab

4. Select the cell containing the title Monthly Household Expenses

5. Press the Bold icon **B**, click the left button on the Office Button

6. Select the Save As icon [Save As], the Save As dialog box appears

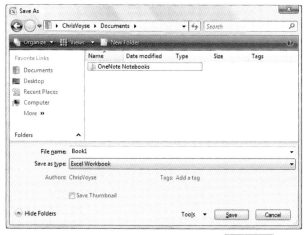

7. Type Expenses in the File name box, select [Save]

8. The Title Bar at the top of the screen now displays the named workbook

Saving a Workbook

There are occasions when a workbook needs to be saved in a different format, for example if a file needs to be saved in an earlier version format, Excel 97-2003.

1. Click on the Office Button   , choose   Save As

2. Alternatively press F12 on the keyboard

3. The Save As dialog box appears

4. In the File name area type Expenses

5. In the Save as type box click on the downward pointing arrow

6. Select Excel 97-2003 workbook, click   Save

```
Excel Workbook
Excel Macro-Enabled Workbook
Excel Binary Workbook
Excel 97-2003 Workbook
XML Data
Single File Web Page
Web Page
Excel Template
```

Figure 7

Opening a Workbook using the Office Button

1. Click on the Office Button

2. The Recent Documents area displays the latest documents used

3. Click with the left   button on the required workbook

4. Alternatively hold down the Alt key, press the letter F

5. Use the → or ↓ arrow keys to highlight the file

6. Press the Enter key to open the workbook

Note: **When opening a file from the recent documents list an error message appears if the file has been renamed, moved or deleted.**

Amending or Deleting Recently Used Files

1. Choose the Office Button

2. Select   Excel Options ,   Advanced

3. The Excel Options dialog box appears

4. Choose the option named Display

5. Select the Number of documents in the Recent Documents list:

Figure 8

6. Type in the number of documents to be displayed, click [OK]

7. To activate the new defaults, click the Office Button

8. Select [New], choose [Create]

Opening a Workbook using the Mouse

1. Press the Office Button , click [Open..], the Open dialog box appears

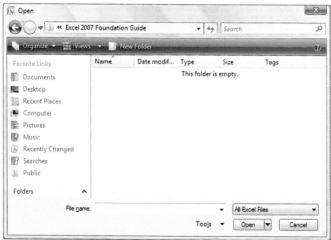

Figure 9

2. Choose [Documents] or the drive that contains the workbook

3. Double click with the left button to open the required folder

4. Or click the left button on the individual workbook, press [Open]

Opening Several Workbooks using the Control Key

1. Press the Office Button ,Click [Open...]

2. Double click with the left button to open the required folder

3. Click the filename once with the left button to select a workbook

4. Hold the [Ctrl] key down to select the next workbook

5. Each selected file is highlighted in blue

6. If a file is selected by mistake click again to deselect

7. Click [Open ▼] to open all the workbooks

Opening Several Workbooks using the Shift Key

1. Press the Office Button ,click [Open...]

2. Double click with the left button to open the required folder

3. Click the left button to select the first workbook

4. Hold the [Shift] key down, click the left button to select the last file

5. All selected files are highlighted in blue

6. Click [Open ▼] to display all the workbooks

Introducing Custom Lists

Why Use a Custom List?

If you need to repeat information on a regular basis creating a Custom List is the best option.

Defining a Custom List

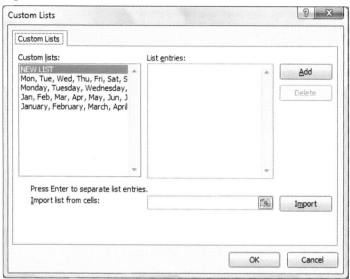

Figure 10

1. Click on the Office Button
2. Select Excel Options, Popular
3. Under the option named Top options for working with Excel
4. Choose Edit Custom Lists...
5. The Custom Lists dialog box appears as shown above
6. The left hand side of the Custom lists dialog box displays the pre set lists
7. To define a new custom list, click with the left button in List entries
8. Type out the list that you want to define
9. Press the Enter key after each list entry
10. When you have finished entering your list, select the Add icon
11. The list is added to the Custom lists area, press OK twice

Exercise 2: - Creating and Deleting a Custom List

The objective of this exercise is to define and reproduce information from a Custom List. Once created the defined list can be reproduced in any worksheet.

Customer Services
Human Resources
Logistics
Payroll
Purchasing
Research and Development

1. Choose the Office Button 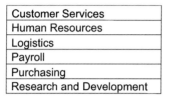 , Excel Options , Popular

2. Select Edit Custom Lists...

3. The left hand Custom lists dialog box displays the pre set lists

4. To define a new custom list click the left ⌐ button in the List entries area

5. Type out the details for each department on a different line

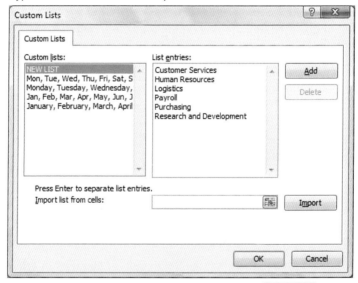

6. When you have finished entering your list select the Add icon

7. The list is added to the Custom lists area

8. Press OK twice

9. Click in a cell in any worksheet and type out Customer Services

10. Move the mouse pointer 🔍 over the bottom right hand corner

11. The white cross ⌖ changes to a thin black cross

12. Click with the left ⌖ button and drag down six cells

13. The information to be placed in the next cell appears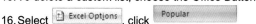

14. Drag over the required cells then release the mouse

15. To delete a custom list, choose the Office Button 🔘

16. Select [Excel Options], click [Popular]

17. Choose [Edit Custom Lists...]

18. In the Custom list area select the list to be deleted

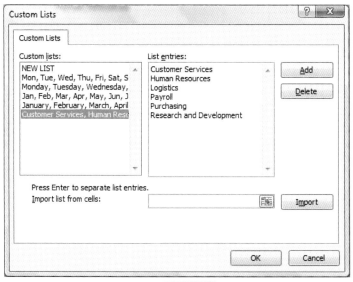

19. The list is highlighted, select the [Delete] icon, select [OK]

20. The list is deleted from the Custom Lists area

21. Select [OK] twice to return to the worksheet

Note: It is not possible to delete the pre set custom lists.

Using the Undo and Redo Facility

When entering information in a cell or a command is used, the information is stored in the memory. The Undo and Redo facility allows a user to go backwards or forwards on a step-by-step basis. The Undo and Redo icons are located on the Quick Access Toolbar located towards the top of the screen.

1. To undo an action click on the Undo icon ↩
2. If you require to undo several steps, click on the downward arrow ▾
3. Highlight over the steps that you want to undo
4. It is possible to go back a step if you have not saved the workbook
5. Repeat the same steps for the Redo icon ↪ ▾

Note: **If you clicked on the downward arrow and selected the stage that you want to go back to it will delete all the steps.**

Entering Simple Formula

In Excel the formula bar automatically resizes to accommodate long or complex formulas.

1. Create the following data

	A	B
1		
2		
3	**Regional Office**	**Sales**
4	Barnsley	26485
5	Derby	14000
6	Doncaster	23675
7	Leeds	34876
8	Leicester	8734
9	Manchester	12398
10	Nottingham	12876
11	Sheffield	3421
12		
13	Total	

Figure 11

2. To add up the sales figures in column B
3. Select the cell where you want the answer to appear
4. All formula starts with equals = and the word sum
5. Type =sum, hold down the Shift key, press the opening bracket sign (
6. Once a bracket is open you can drag over the cells you want to add up
7. The cells are automatically referenced in the formula
8. Creating your formula in this way means less typing and fewer mistakes

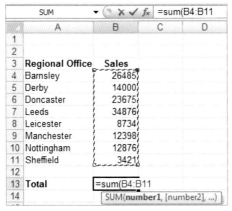

Figure 12

9. If you open a bracket you must close a bracket ⬚

10. Alternatively type =SUM(B4:B11) or
    =SUM(B4+B5+B6+B7+B8+B9+B10+B11)

11. If you are using just one set of brackets and forget to close the bracket at
    the end of the formula, Excel will add this automatically

12. To complete the formula click on the blue tick ✓

13. Or press the [Enter] key on the keyboard

14. The result displayed in cell B13 is 136465

15. Save the Workbook

Using the AutoSum Icon

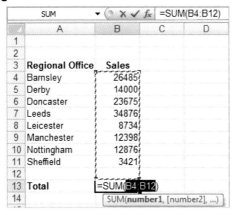

Figure 13

1. Select the Formulas Tab

2. Click in cell B13, select Σ from the Function Library Group

3. The formula appears =sum(B4:B12)

4. Cell B12 contains no information, however the AutoSum feature thinks you want to add up all the cells above B13

5. However, in this instance cell B12 **does not** want to be selected

6. A moving line appears around the area Excel thinks you want to add up

7. Move the mouse pointer ⟍ into the middle of cell B4

8. Click and hold down the left button, drag to cell B11

9. A line appears around the selected text, click on the blue tick ✓

10. Alternatively press the Enter key on the keyboard

11. B13 contains the result 136465

Note: If you required a formula that needed a blank line to separate the total from the data, create the formula result first then insert a row above the total.

Using Multiplication

	A	B	C	D
1		Monthly Salary	Tax	Net Income
2	Simon Cave	£3,500.00		
3	Paul Spandler	£1,210.00		
4	Joan Wood	£780.00		
5	Alison Muratore	£930.00		

Figure 14

The following steps display an easy way to create the multiplication formula. To multiply Excel uses the asterisks * button. Remember all formula starts with the equals sign =.

1. Create the above table, select cell C2, press =

2. Click in cell B2, the reference is displayed in the formula bar

3. Alternatively type out B2

4. Use the multiplication sign * and type the TAX rate (in this instance 20%)

5. The correct formula is SUM ▼ X ✓ fx =B2*20%

6. Click on the blue tick ✓ in the formula bar to remain in the cell

7. The information displayed in cell C2 should be £700.00

8. In cell C2, click on the black cross fill handle in the bottom right hand corner

9. Drag over cells C3, C4 and C5

10. This formula is a relative reference; this means the formula is relative to each column and each row

C5			f_x	=B5*20%	
	A	B	C	D	
1		Monthly Salary	Tax	Net Income	
2	Simon Cave	£3,500.00	£700.00		
3	Paul Spandler	£1,210.00	£242.00		
4	Joan Wood	£780.00	£156.00		
5	Alison Muratore	£930.00	£186.00		

Figure 15

11. The result appears in cells C3 to C5

Using Subtraction

	A	B	C	D
1		Monthly Salary	Tax	Net Income
2	Simon Cave	£3,500.00	£700.00	
3	Paul Spandler	£1,210.00	£242.00	
4	Joan Wood	£780.00	£156.00	
5	Alison Muratore	£930.00	£186.00	

Figure 16

1. Click in cell D2, all formula starts with , type B2-C2

2. Or press the = key, click in cell B2, press the - sign and click in C2

3. The cell reference is placed in the formula bar, press the Enter key

D2			f_x	=B2-C2	
	A	B	C	D	
1		Monthly Salary	Tax	Net Income	
2	Simon Cave	£3,500.00	£700.00	£2,800.00	
3	Paul Spandler	£1,210.00	£242.00		
4	Joan Wood	£780.00	£156.00		
5	Alison Muratore	£930.00	£186.00		

Figure 17

4. Move the mouse pointer over the bottom right hand corner of D2

5. Click with the left button on the black fill handle, drag down to cell D5

6. The results appear in cells D3 to D5

Using Division

Excel uses the forward slash key 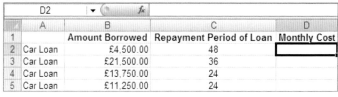 to divide information.

	A	B	C	D
1		Amount Borrowed	Repayment Period of Loan	Monthly Cost
2	Car Loan	£4,500.00	48	
3	Car Loan	£21,500.00	36	
4	Car Loan	£13,750.00	24	
5	Car Loan	£11,250.00	24	

Figure 18

1. Create the following table

2. Select cell D2, press ⌐=⌐

3. Click in cell B2 or type B2 in the formula, press ⌐/⌐

4. Click in cell C2 or type C2 [SUM ▼ x ✔ fx =B2/C2]

5. Press the ⌐Enter⌐ key

6. The result in cell D2 should be £93.75

7. Use the black fill handle to drag the results for D3, D4 and D5

Using the Functions Sum, Min, Max, Average, Count

Excel 2007 lets you quickly calculate statistical information, for example minimum, maximum, average and count. The function name used to add information together is **sum**.

	A	B	C	D	E
1		£25,678	£5,679	£25,762	£5,643
2		£87,905	£765	£86,257	£79,233
3		£567,900	£46,870	£67,543	£29,858
4		£76,549	£6,874	£26,718	£54,289
5		£79,567	£89,643	£79,567	£67,528
6					
7	Total	£837,599	£149,831	£285,847	£236,551
8	Min				
9	Max				
10	Average				
11	Count				

Figure 19

1. Select a new workbook, type out the information in Rows 1 - 5 shown above

2. Type the words in cells A7 to A11

3. Click with the left ⌐🖰⌐ button in cell B7

4. Create the formula in cell B7, copy it across to cells C7, D7 and E7

5. Select cell B8, all formula starts with =

6. Instead of using the word Sum use the word Min

7. Insert the bracket sign (

8. Click the left button in cell B1, a moving line appears around the cell

9. Hold the left button down and drag down to cell B5

SUM		▼	⨉ ✔ ƒx	=Min(B1:B5)
	A	B	C	D	E
1		£25,678	£5,679	£25,762	£5,643
2		£87,905	£765	£86,257	£79,233
3		£567,900	£46,870	£67,543	£29,858
4		£76,549	£6,874	£26,718	£54,289
5		£79,567	£89,643	£79,567	£67,528
6					
7	Total	£837,599	£149,831	£285,847	£236,551
8	Min	=Min(B1:B5)			
9	Max				
10	Average				
11	Count				

Figure 20

10. The formula states =Min(B1:B5 in the cell and the formula bar

11. Close the bracket sign)

12. Click on the blue tick ✔ to remain in cell B8

13. Move the mouse pointer ↖ to the bottom right hand corner of cell B8

14. Use the black fill handle, click the left button and drag over C8 to E8

15. Release the left button, the formula is copied to the cells

16. Now create the formula for the Rows 9 to 11

	A	B	C	D	E
1		£25,678	£5,679	£25,762	£5,643
2		£87,905	£765	£86,257	£79,233
3		£567,900	£46,870	£67,543	£29,858
4		£76,549	£6,874	£26,718	£54,289
5		£79,567	£89,643	£79,567	£67,528
6					
7	Total	£837,599	£149,831	£285,847	£236,551
8	Min	£25,678	£765	£25,762	£5,643
9	Max	£567,900	£89,643	£86,257	£79,233
10	Average	£167,520	£29,966	£57,169	£47,310
11	Count	5	5	5	5

Figure 21

17. Save the workbook as Working with Total Min Max Average and Count

Using the Insert Functions Feature

If a user was working in a workbook and forgot the function name of a formula, Excel provides a quick and easy access.

	A	B	C	D	E
1		£25,678	£5,679	£25,762	£5,643
2		£87,905	£765	£86,257	£79,233
3		£567,900	£46,870	£67,543	£29,858
4		£76,549	£6,874	£26,718	£54,289
5		£79,567	£89,643	£79,567	£67,528
6					
7	Total	£837,599	£149,831	£285,847	£236,551
8	Min	£25,678	£765	£25,762	£5,643
9	Max				
10	Average				
11	Count				

Figure 22

1. Using the above table, click on the ⌐Formulas¬ Tab

2. Click with the left button in cell B9 where the results are to appear

3. Choose 𝑓𝑥 Insert Function from the Function Library Group

4. The Insert Function dialog box appears

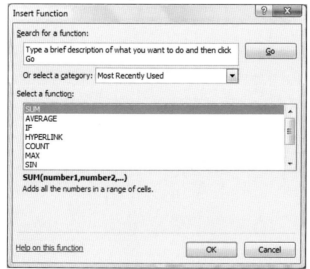

Figure 23

5. Under the heading **S**earch for a function, type max

6. Press [Go]

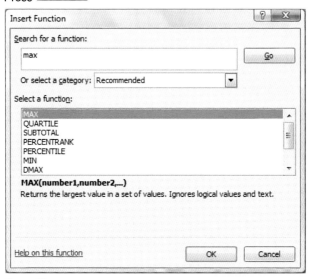

Figure 24

7. The description is displayed in the Select a functio**n** box

8. Click [OK], the Function Arguments dialog box appears

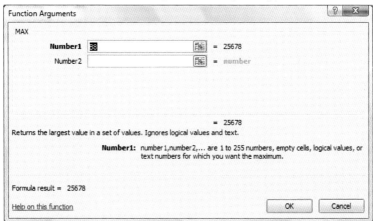

Figure 25

9. Select the dialog box icon 📷

10. Click in the centre of cell B1 and drag to cell B5

11. =MAX(B1:B5) is displayed in the Formula Bar

Function Arguments

B1:B5

Figure 26

12. Select the dialog box icon 🔲 again

13. Click ⬚ OK ⬚ to display the results

Exercise 3: - Consolidation Working with Formulas

	A	B	C	D	E
1	Name	Salary	Monthly	Tax	Total
2	Wright	£16,570.00	£1,380.83	£296.88	£1,083.95
3	Broad	£57,000.00	£4,750.00	£1,021.25	
4	Parratt	£85,600.00	£7,133.33	£1,533.67	
5	Martin	£16,000.00	£1,333.33	£286.67	
6	Christian	£14,750.00	£1,229.17	£264.27	
7	Nichols	£17,800.00	£1,483.33	£318.92	
8	Layne	£16,870.00	£1,405.83	£302.25	
9	Kirby	£13,200.00	£1,100.00	£236.50	
10	Roberts	£22,000.00	£1,833.33	£394.17	
11	Davidson	£11,250.00	£937.50	£201.56	
12					
13	Totals				
14	Maximum				
15	Minimum				
16	Average				
17	Count				

1. Open a new workbook
2. Create the information shown in columns A and B above
3. In cell C1 type Monthly, in D1 type Tax and in E1 type Total
4. Click in cell B13, create a formula to calculate the total salary
5. Create individual formulas for cell B14 to B17
6. Select C2, create a formula to calculate the monthly salary
7. Use the fill handle to copy the relative formula to C11
8. Using a tax rate of 21.5% create a formula to display the monthly tax paid by each person
9. In column E work out the monthly take home pay for each person
10. Save the exercise as Working with Different Formulas

Moving Information in a Worksheet

Moving information in Excel is easy, to move information in cell A6 to B2

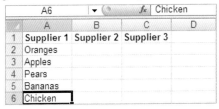

Figure 27

1. Type the above table in a new worksheet

2. Select cell A6, choose the ⌗Home⌗ Tab, click on the Cut icon ✄ Cut

3. A moving dotted line appears around the selected cell

4. Click in cell B2, select the Paste icon 📋

5. The information from cell A6 is moved to cell B2

Note: To use the right mouse button follow the same steps selecting the required icon.

Using Keyboard Shortcuts to Move Information

1. Select cell A6

2. Hold down the ⌗Ctrl⌗ key, select ⌗X⌗

3. A moving dotted line appears around the selected cell

4. Click in cell B2

5. Hold down the ⌗Ctrl⌗ key, select ⌗V⌗

6. The information from cell A6 is moved to cell B2

Using the Drag and Drop Feature to Move Information

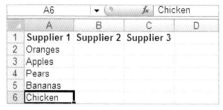

Figure 28

1. Select cell A6

2. Move the mouse pointer ⬉ over the left hand corner of the cell A6

3. A pointing arrow appears

4. Click and hold down the left 🖱 button

5. The left hand corner of the status bar states Drag to move cell contents

6. Keeping the left 🖱 button down, drag to the new destination

7. Release the left 🖱 button in cell B2

8. The information from cell A6 is moved to cell B2

Copying Information in a Worksheet

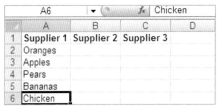

Figure 29

Copying information in cell A6 to B2

1. Select cell A6, press the Home Tab

2. Choose the Copy icon Copy

3. A moving dotted line appears around the selected cell

4. Click in cell B2, select the Paste icon

5. The information from cell A6 is moved to cell B2

6. Click with your left button to select the new cell

7. Select the Paste icon

8. The information from cell A6 is copied to the new cell B2

9. The moving dotted line still appears

10. To switch off the dotted line, press Enter or the Esc key on the keyboard

Using Keyboard Shortcuts to Copy Information

1. Select cell A6

2. Hold down the Ctrl key, select C

3. A moving dotted line appears around the selected cell

4. Click with your left button to select the new cell B2

5. Hold down the Ctrl key and select V

6. The information from cell A6 is copied to cell B2

7. To switch off the dotted line, press Enter or the Esc key

Using the Drag and Drop Feature to Copy Information

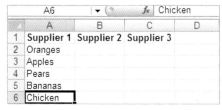

Figure 30

1. Select cell A6

2. Move the mouse pointer ↖ over the left hand corner of the cell A6

3. Hold down the [Ctrl] key and the left ⌐🖱 button

4. A plus sign + appears above the white arrow when the [Ctrl] key is down

5. The bottom left hand corner of the Status Bar states Drag to copy cell contents

6. Drag with the mouse pointer ↖ to the new location

7. Release the left ⌐🖱 button before the [Ctrl] key

8. The information in cell A6 has been copied to the new cell

BODMAS

What is BODMAS?

BODMAS is the mathematical method that Excel 2007 uses to calculate a formula.

Name	Description	Symbol
B	Brackets	( )
O	To The Power of	^
D	Division	/
M	Multiplication	*
A	Addition	+
S	Subtraction	-

Figure 31

Excel always uses the BODMAS rule to work out information in brackets before it completes the multiplication part of the formula.

To work out the answer to "what is 5+2*10?"

Using the BODMAS rule, Excel will work out the multiplication part of the formula before the 5+2, however if the formula is =(5+2)*10 then Excel will work out the information in brackets first and then multiply the result by 10.

Different Types of References

Reference	Description of Reference
$A$1	Defines always look at Column A and Row 1
A$1	Defines always look at Row 1 but not Column A
$A1	Defines always look at Column A but not Row 1
A1	This is a normal cell reference

Figure 32

Excel uses four different types of references when working with formula.   To change the reference you need to type in a formula.

1. Select the cell that needs to be changed

2. Click on the cell reference in the Formula Bar

3. Press F4 slowly four times

4. The reference goes through the four different cell reference options

5. Select the reference required

6. Alternatively type out the reference

Absolute Cell Referencing

Absolute Cell Referencing saves time when working in Excel, for example if the VAT rate or a commission rate has been changed, Absolute Cell Referencing is a quick method of changing the reference that the formula is working to. The formula automatically updates information referenced in the cell.

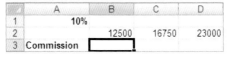

Figure 33

1. Type the above table in a new worksheet

2. Create the formula =B2*A1, Excel works out 10% of 12500

3. In a relative formula you could drag across using the fill handle and if applied the results would be cell C3 zero and cell D3 zero

4. That is because no absolute cell reference has been applied

5. (In the above example) absolute means "when applying the formula always look at cell A1"

6. To make a cell reference absolute use the following steps

7. Select cell B3

8. Click in the Formula Bar

9. After =B2*A1, a flashing cursor appears

10. Press F4, dollar signs appear around A1

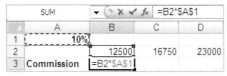

Figure 34

11. Think of the dollar sign as saying "always look at Column A and always look at Row 1"

12. Select the blue tick ✓ to update the formula and remain in the cell

13. Use the fill handle to drag across C3 and D3

14. The formula in cell C3 is =C2*$A$1

15. The formula in cell D3 is =D2*$A$1

Formatting Options

Formatting is a quick way to apply different layouts or designs to your worksheet. In Excel 2007, the Ribbon has seven Tabs; each Tab groups together related items that enable the user to carry out a series of commands.

The Font Group Icons

Icon	Descriptive Prompt
Arial	Font Face
10	Font Size
A	Increase Font Size
A	Decrease Font Size
B	**Makes selected text and numbers bold**
I	*Makes selected text and numbers italic*
U	<u>Makes selected text and numbers underlined</u>
D	<u>Makes selected text and numbers double underlined</u>
	Borders
	Fill Colour
A	Font Colour
	Click the left button to open the Format Cells dialog box

Figure 35

Formatting Cells using the Font Group

1. Select the Home Tab to display the Font Group

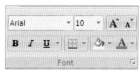

Figure 36

2. Select the cells that require formatting

3. Change the font by clicking on the Font Face icon Arial

4. A drop down menu displaying the Theme Fonts appears

5. Change the name of the font to Arial or a font of your choice

6. Click on the Font Size icon 10, change the font size

The Alignment Group Icons

Icon	Descriptive Prompt
≡	Top Align
≡	Middle Align
≡	Bottom Align
≫ ▾	Orientation rotate text
≣	Aligns the selected text, numbers, or objects to the left
≣	Centres the selected text, numbers, or objects
≣	Aligns the selected text, numbers, or objects to the right
≢	Decrease Indent
≢	Increase Indent
▤	Wrap Text
▦ ▾	Merge and Centre
▤	Merge Across
▥	Merge Cells
▦	Unmerge Cells
▣	Click the left ⌖ button to open the Format Cells dialog box

Figure 37

Formatting Cells using the Alignment Group

1. Select the ⌗ Home ⌗ Tab to display the Alignment Group

Figure 38

2. Select the cells that require formatting
3. Change the alignment by clicking on the Align Text Command icon ≣

The Number Group Icons

Icon	Descriptive Prompt
General ▼	Number Format
🔲 ▼	Currency
%	Percentage Style
,	Comma Style
←.0 .00	Increase Decimal
.00 →.0	Decrease Decimal
🔲	Use the left 🖱 button to open the Format Cells dialog box

Figure 39

Formatting Cells using the Number Group

1. Select the   Home   Tab to display the Number Group

Figure 40

2. Select the cells that require formatting

3. Change the numbering by clicking on the Comma Style icon [,]

Using the Home Tab to Create Borders

The Borders icon adds or removes borders around selected cells. To display the different types of borders

1. Highlight the cells that require a border

2. Select the ⌞ Home ⌟ Tab

3. Click on the More Borders icon ⊞ ▾ in the Font Group

4. The Borders menu appears

Figure 41

5. Choose ⊞ More Borders...

6. The Format Cells dialog box appears with the ⌞ Border ⌟ Tab selected

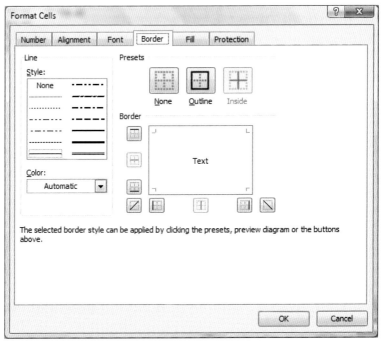

Figure 42

7. Choose the **S**tyle of line and **C**olour required

8. Select **O**utline or Inside border

9. Click on the [Fill] Tab

10. Select Background **C**olour and choose the colour required

11. Click [OK]

12. To remove a border, highlight the cells

13. Click on the More Borders icon [⊞▾]

14. Select [⊞ No Border]

15. To remove the fill colour, highlight the cells

16. Click on the Fill Colour icon [▨▾]

17. Select [No Fill]

Formatting Cells using the Home Tab

When using Excel 2007, it is possible to format a worksheet using the Home Tab and by selecting the cells to be changed. You must select the cell(s) before you can format information.

1. Highlight the cells to be formatted

2. Select the Tab

3. Choose  from the Cells Grouping

4. The Cell Size menu appears

Figure 43

5. Select 📄 Format Cells...

6. The Format Cells dialog box appears

7. Click on the Number Tab

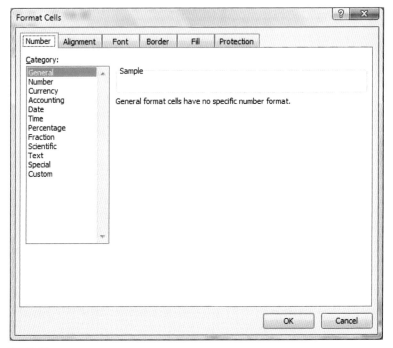

Figure 44

8. Select **C**ategory and choose the required format

9. Click [OK]

Aligning Information using the Home Tab

1. Highlight the cells to be formatted

2. Select the Home Tab

3. Choose Format from the Cells Grouping

4. Select Format Cells...

5. Click on the Alignment Tab

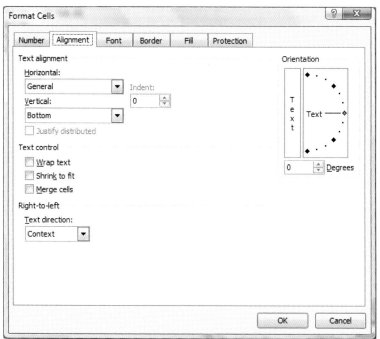

Figure 45

6. Change the **H**orizontal and **V**ertical options to Centre

7. Orientation enables 'text' information to be displayed at an angle

8. Change the Text control to either **W**rap text, Shrin**k** to fit or **M**erge cells

9. Click OK

Formatting Text using the Home Tab and Font Grouping

1. Highlight the cells to be formatted

2. Select the Tab

3. Choose ![Format] from the Cells Grouping

4. Select 🗗 Format Cells...

5. Click on the | Font | Tab

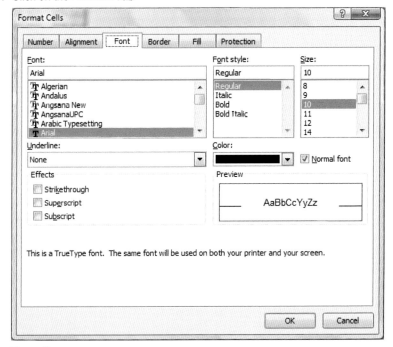

Figure 46

6. Choose <u>F</u>ont and select the type of font required

7. Repeat these steps to change the F<u>o</u>nt style, <u>S</u>ize, <u>U</u>nderline and <u>C</u>olour

8. Stri<u>k</u>ethrough, Sup<u>e</u>rscript and Su<u>b</u>script are special alignment options

9. The selected formatting options are displayed in the Preview area

10. Click [OK] to apply the changes

Formatting Cells using the Fill Tab

The [Fill] Tab sets the background colour of a highlighted area.

1. To format cells using the [Fill] Tab, select the cells to be formatted

2. Choose the [Home] Tab

3. Select  from the Cells Grouping, click 🖳 Format Cells...

4. The Format Cells dialog box appears

5. Click on the [Fill] Tab

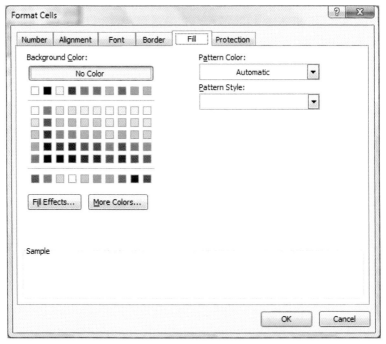

Figure 47

6. Choose Background **C**olour, select the background colour from the menu

7. Follow the same steps to select a P**a**ttern Colour and/or a **P**attern Style

8. The selection can be seen in the Sample area

9. Click [OK] to apply the changes

Format Painter Icon

Using the Format Painter icon [Format Painter] allows users to copy formatting from one place and apply it to another.

1. Click in the cell with the format you want to copy

2. Select the [Home] Tab

3. Move the mouse pointer ↖ to [Format Painter]

4. Double click the [Format Painter] to apply the format to multiple cells

5. When the Format Painter icon is switched on it is indented

6. When moving over the cell you will see a white cross and brush

7. A dotted line appears around the original cell

8. Click with the left 🖱 button in the cell you want to apply the format

9. The format of the cell is changed to that of the original cell

10. Switch the Format Painter off by selecting the icon again

11. The dotted line disappears when the facility is switched off

12. To apply a format to one cell

13. Select [Format Painter] once

14. When the cell is selected the Format Painter automatically switches itself off

Using the Page Layout Tab

The Page Setup Grouping includes quick and easy commands that allow changes to be made to margins, orientation, size, print area, breaks, background and print titles.

1. Select the Page Layout Tab, the Page Setup grouping is displayed

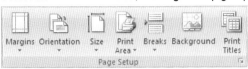

Figure 48

2. Choose Orientation, select Landscape

3. Select [Size], the size menu appears

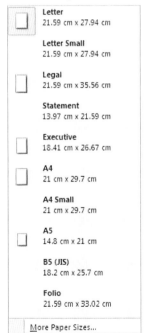

Figure 49

4. Select the required paper size

5. Select the Office Button

6. Choose ,

7. Click on the ![Close Print Preview] icon

8. Or press [Ctrl] [F2] to preview your worksheet

9. Press the [Esc] key on the keyboard to return to the worksheet

10. Alternatively click with the left button on the dialog box launcher

11. The Page Setup dialog box appears

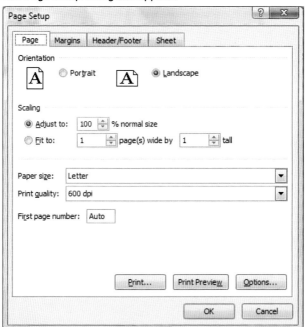

Figure 50

To Change Margin Sizes

1. Using the [Page Layout] Tab, select [Margins ▼], the margins menu is displayed

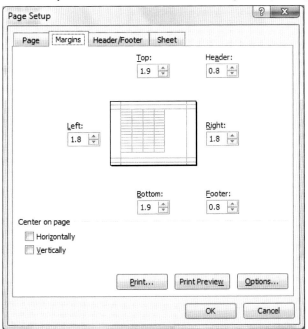

Normal		
Top: 1.91 cm	Bottom: 1.91 cm	
Left: 1.78 cm	Right: 1.78 cm	
Header: 0.76 cm	Footer: 0.76 cm	

Figure 51

2. Change the margins by selecting Normal, Wide or Narrow

3. Alternatively choose [Custom Margins...], the Page Setup dialog box appears

Figure 52

4. Select the [Margins] Tab

5. Change the default settings **T**op, **B**ottom, **L**eft and **R**ight

6. Click on the Hori**z**ontally and **V**ertically options to centre on the page

7. The Header and Footer margins can also be changed from this screen

8. Click [OK]

Header and Footer Options

1. Using the ⌐Page Layout¬ Tab, select

2. Choose ⌐Custom Margins...¬, the Page Setup dialog box appears

3. Select the ⌐Header/Footer¬ Tab

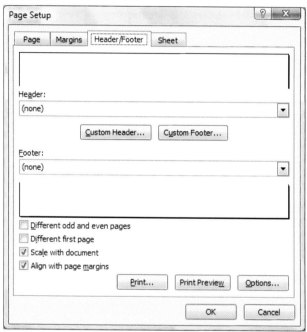

Figure 53

4. The He**a**der and **F**ooter boxes provide a preview of both areas

Figure 54

5. Choose the downward pointing arrows to view the standard pre set options

6. The preview area displays the selected option

7. Click on the downward pointing arrow to return to the ⌐Header/Footer¬ Tab

8. To create a Custom Header, select [Custom Header...]

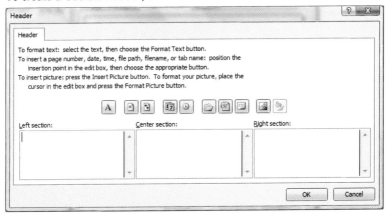

Figure 55

9. The Header and Footer icons are shown below

Header and Footer Options	
Icon	**Descriptive Prompt**
A	Define font size and style options
#	Inserts the Page Number
⊞	Inserts Number of Pages
🗓	Insert Date
🕐	Insert Time
📁	File and Path
📄	Filename
🗒	Tab Name
🖼	Picture
✋	Format Picture Options
OK	Accept Changes and go back to Page Setup options
Cancel	Go back to the Page Set Up Options

Figure 56

10. Create the Header and Footer information, click [OK]

11. The [Custom Footer...] icon enables the Footer area to be created

12. Create the Footer information, click [OK] twice

13. To preview the Header and Footer information press [Ctrl] and [F2]

Exercise 4: - Creating Header and Footer Information

1. Open the workbook named Working with Different Formulas
2. Create a centre heading using the name of a school or organisation
3. Select the Custom Footer, in the Centre section create Page 1 of 1
4. Preview your worksheet to view the changes
5. Save the Workbook

To Define a Print Area

1. Using the `Page Layout` Tab, select the Print Titles icon
2. Or click on the dialog box launcher to bring up the Page Setup grouping
3. Select the `Sheet` Tab, click on the Print area icon

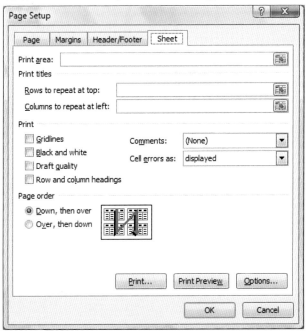

Figure 57

4. The Page Setup Print area: box is displayed

Figure 58

5. Highlight the cells, the absolute references will appear in the print area
6. A dotted line appears around the selected area
7. Click on the Print area icon to close the Print area window
8. Select `Print Preview`, choose print

To Clear a Print Area

1. Select the  Tab

2. Click on the Print Area icon

3. Select

Note: If a print area is defined and a further area needs to be selected; select the additional area and click the print area icon. Select the add to print area icon to update the print area selection.

Print Preview

1. Click on the Office Button

2. Choose

3. Click on the zoom icon to zoom in and out of a page

4. By moving the mouse pointer over the page a magnifying glass appears

5. Click with the left button to zoom in and out of a page

6. Select Next Page or Previous Page to view multiple pages

7. Using the left button move the vertical scroll bar to view the page

8. Preview: Page 5 of 9 is displayed in the Status Bar at the bottom of the screen

9. Click on the Show Margins icon to display or adjust the margins

10. Select Print to open the Print dialog box

Using the Spell Feature

The Spell Feature checks the text in a document for incorrect spelling using the standard built in dictionary that can also be customised.

1. Select the | Review | Tab, choose Spelling or press F7
2. The spelling dialog box appears if there are spelling errors in the text

Figure 59

3. The suggestions area gives alternative spellings

4. Choose the correct spelling, click | Change | to replace the word

5. To add a new word to the dictionary, click | Add to Dictionary |

6. The spelling facility continues until the end of the worksheet

7. Once the spell check has been completed the following dialog box appears

Figure 60

8. Press | OK | to return to the worksheet

Printing

1. Choose the Office Button 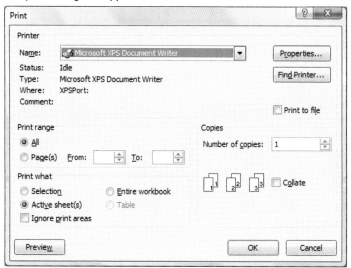, select

2. The print dialog box appears

Figure 61

3. The active printer is shown

4. To change the printer click on the Na**me** box

5. Use the downward arrow to select the required printer

6. Select the Print range required

7. Choose the Number of **c**opies required, default is 1 copy

8. Tick C**o**llate if the worksheets are to be collated

9. Select Acti**v**e Sheet(s), or select the **E**ntire workbook if this is required

10. Click [Preview] to check the worksheet before printing

11. Select

12. Alternatively [Alt] [F] [P] displays the Print dialog box

Introduction to Simple Charts

Excel 2007 allows the user to create a chart from information that the user has been working with and displays this data graphically in an embedded chart that can be placed and saved on the same sheet as your data, or on a chart sheet that displays the data separately from the data sheet. Both the embedded chart and the chart sheet are automatically updated when data on the worksheet is changed.

Different Parts of a Chart

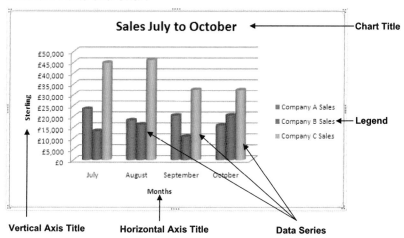

Figure 62

Chart Title

The chart title identifies the name of the chart.

Legend

The Legend defines the symbols used in each data series in the chart.

Vertical Axis

Indicates the unit of measurement used in the chart.

Horizontal Axis

Indicates the categories used in the chart.

Data Series

The Data Series represents a group of data incorporated in a row or column from an Excel worksheet. A chart consists of one or more data series.

A chart can be resized using the mouse by dragging from any of the corner points of the chart.

Creating a Simple Chart

1. Create the following table

	A	B	C	D	E	F
1		July	August	September	October	Total
2	Company A Sales	£23,400	£18,200	£20,421	£15,876	£77,897
3	Company B Sales	£13,275	£16,320	£10,745	£20,486	£60,826
4	Company C Sales	£44,739	£46,100	£32,400	£30,200	£153,439

Figure 63

2. Select cells A1 to E4 using the left button

3. Choose the | Insert | Tab

4. Select the ![Column] icon from the Charts Grouping

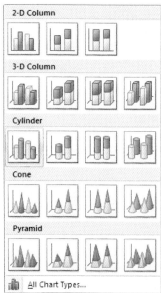

Figure 64

5. Select Clustered Cylinder

6. The chart appears on the worksheet as shown below

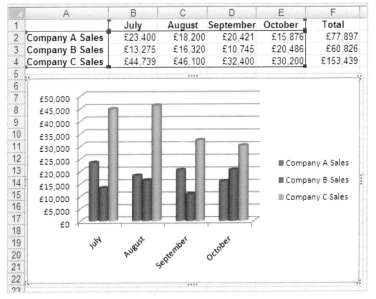

	A	B	C	D	E	F
1		July	August	September	October	Total
2	Company A Sales	£23,400	£18,200	£20,421	£15,876	£77,897
3	Company B Sales	£13,275	£16,320	£10,745	£20,486	£60,826
4	Company C Sales	£44,739	£46,100	£32,400	£30,200	£153,439

Figure 65

7. To add, remove or update data in the chart

8. Click in the cell where information is to be added, removed or updated

9. Type in the changes, press the Enter key

10. The chart is updated automatically

11. To add a heading, legend, category and value data to the chart

12. Click with the left button in the chart area to activate the chart tools

13. Choose the Design Tab

14. Select the Chart Layouts Grouping

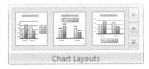

Figure 66

15. Use the downward pointing arrow ⬇ to expand the menu box

16. Choose Layout 9

Figure 67

17. Click on Chart Title in the chart

18. Change the title to Sales July to October, click outside the Chart Title area

19. Click on the horizontal axis title, type Months, click outside the Horizontal Axis Title area

20. Type Sterling in the vertical axis box

Figure 68

21. Save the chart as My Simple Chart

Adding New Data to a Chart

1. Select the original worksheet My Simple Chart

2. To add the figures for November

3. Click on column heading F

4. Select the Home Tab, click [Insert] from the Cells Grouping

5. The new column is inserted

6. Click in cell F1 type November as the heading

7. In cell F2 type £16,000

8. In cell F3 type £25,125

9. In cell F4 type £31,965

10. Change the chart title to Sales July to November

11. Click in the Chart Area, a blue border appears around the figures July to October

	A	B	C	D	E	F	G
1		July	August	September	October	November	Total
2	Company A Sales	£23,400	£18,200	£20,421	£15,876	£16,000	£93,897
3	Company B Sales	£13,275	£16,320	£10,745	£20,486	£25,125	£85,951
4	Company C Sales	£44,739	£46,100	£32,400	£32,200	£31,965	£187,404

Figure 69

12. Move the mouse pointer on the blue square in column E

13. Click with the left button and drag to include the figures for November

14. The chart is updated automatically as displayed on the next page

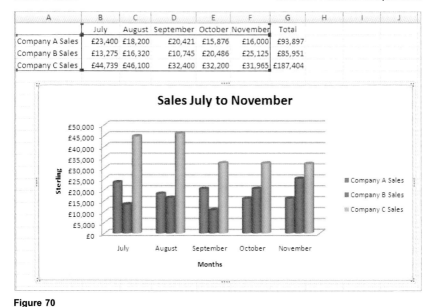

Figure 70

Changing the Style of a Chart

1. Click in the chart, select the Design Tab, choose chart styles
2. Select the style required by using the downward pointing arrow
3. The chart is updated automatically

Figure 71

To Change the Type of Chart

1. Click in the chart, select the Design Tab

2. Choose Change Chart Type in the Type Groupings

3. The Change Chart Type dialog box appears

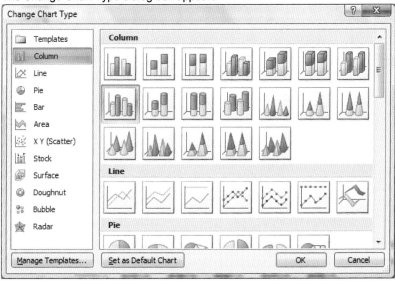

Figure 72

4. Select the chart type required, press OK

Figure 73

Printing a Chart Sheet

1. Click with the left 🖱 button to select the chart
2. Select the Office Button
3. Choose 🖨 Print ▸ 🔍 **Print Preview** Preview and make changes to pages before printing.
4. Select Page Setup , choose the Header/Footer Tab
5. Create a Custom Header... and Custom Footer...
6. Click OK , select Print
7. Save the workbook

Exercise 5: - Create a Chart within a Worksheet

Using the data in the previous section update the chart within the worksheet.

1. Change the chart title to read Company Sales July to December
2. Add the December figures as follows:
3. Company A £25,568
4. Company B £30,765
5. Company C £34,236
6. Update the Totals
7. Print the chart to include the figures for July to December
8. Save the workbook

Section 2: Intermediate Level Objectives

- Naming a Worksheet and Navigation

- Analysing Information in Different Worksheets

- Working with Multiple Sheets

- Generate 3-D Formula

- Freezing Panes and Split Windows

- Saving Workbooks in Different Formats

- Working with Different Charts

- Review of BODMAS

- Vertical and Horizontal Lookup Functions

- Inserting Comments

- Password Protection

- Filtering Data

Note: If you are working in Windows XP instead of Windows Vista, dialog boxes may look different but function in a similar way.

Naming a Worksheet and Navigation

Excel opens three worksheets in a workbook by default. To open more worksheets:

1. Click on the Office Button 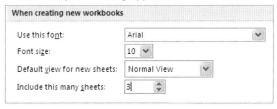 select ⬚ Excel Options
2. The Excel Options dialog appears

Figure 74

3. Choose the option: When creating new workbooks
4. Select: Include this many <u>s</u>heets
5. Type in the number of sheets required or use the arrow keys

Figure 75

6. Press [OK]
7. To display the new default number of worksheets
8. Click the Office Button, select [New]
9. Choose [Create], the new default worksheets appear

Inserting Worksheets

1. Open a new workbook to bring up the 5 sheets

Figure 76

2. Click on the Insert Worksheet icon
3. The new active sheet appears to the right of the previously selected sheet

Sheet5 **Sheet6**

Figure 77

4. To delete a worksheet

5. Click with the right 🖱 button over the worksheet to be deleted

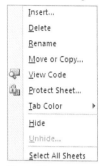

Figure 78

6. Select <u>D</u>elete

To View Unseen Worksheets

If worksheets are not displayed

1. Select the ⏮ icon with the left 🖱 button to display Sheet 1

2. Choose the ⏮ icon to display the last sheet in the workbook

3. Click the ◀▶ icons to display the concealed worksheets

To View Sheet Tabs

1. Using the horizontal scroll bar

Figure 79

2. Move the mouse pointer ▷ over the left hand side of the arrow ▐◀

3. A black vertical double line appears with arrows each side of the lines

4. Click and hold down the left 🖱 button and drag to the right

5. The concealed worksheets are displayed

To Rename a Worksheet

1. Double click with the left 🖱 button on Sheet 1

2. The sheet name is highlighted **Sheet1**

3. Type the new name for the sheet, maximum of 31 characters

Rename a Worksheet using the Right Mouse Button

1. Move the white arrow over Sheet 2

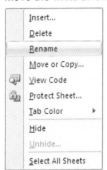

Figure 80

2. Press the right button, select ⬚ Rename
3. The sheet is highlighted **Sheet2**
4. Rename the sheet, press **Enter** to display the new name

To Move a Worksheet

1. Click and hold down the left button on Sheet 1

Sheet1 Sheet2 Sheet3 Sheet4 Sheet5

Figure 81

2. A downward pointing black arrow appears on the sheet tab
3. Hold down the left button, use the arrow as a guide
4. This displays where the new sheet will be positioned
5. Drag Sheet 1 to its new position after Sheet 3
6. Let go of the left button, the sheet has moved to its new position
7. Move Sheet 1 back to its original position

Move or Copy a Worksheet

1. Select the sheet tab to be moved or copied using the left button
2. Click with the right button, select Move or Copy...

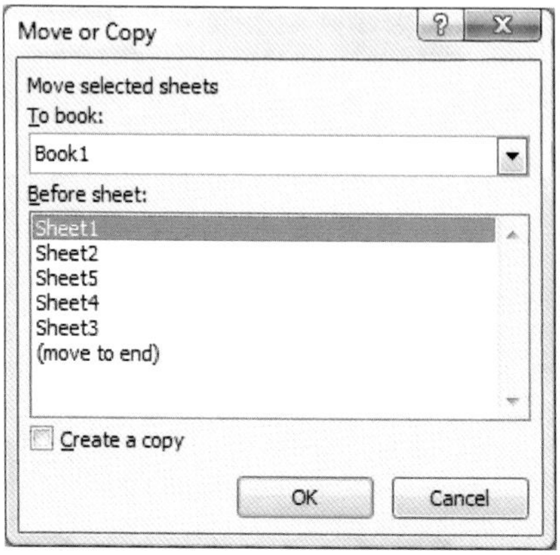

Figure 82

3. Choose the location where the selected sheet needs to be moved to
4. To create a copy, click with the left button on Create a copy
5. Click OK

Note: To move or copy a new workbook or an active workbook that is opened select the arrow in the To book: area.

Applying Colours to Worksheet Tabs

1. Select a sheet tab to apply a colour

2. Click with the right button, choose Tab Color ▶

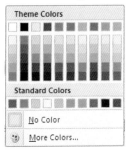

Figure 83

3. Select the required colour
4. The chosen colour is displayed under the sheet tab name Sheet4
5. Select a different tab, the new colour Sheet4 is displayed

Working with Multiple Worksheets

Excel allows a number of sheets to be selected using the left button. If you are creating a number of sheets using the same headings, highlight the sheets concerned, type the headings. The formatting will be applied to all the selected sheets.

1. Click on the tab named Sheet 1

2. Hold down the Ctrl key and click on Sheet 3 and Sheet 5

3. [Group] appears in the title bar at the top of the screen

4. The word group identifies that more than one sheet has been selected

5. Type in cell A1 - Smart PC Guides

6. Widen column A

7. To deselect the group

8. Click with the right button on any sheet tab

9. Select Ungroup Sheets

10. The group name disappears

11. Smart PC Guides appears on Sheets 3 and 5

Note: To select a group of sheets next to each other, click on the first sheet, select Shift before clicking on the last sheet. All the sheets are selected and the Title Bar displays the Group option.

To Delete Worksheets

1. Click with the right 🖱 button over the sheet tab to be deleted
2. Select ⌊ <u>Delete</u> ⌋
3. The sheet is deleted from the workbook

To Print Multiple Worksheets

1. Select the sheets that require printing
2. The [Group] selection is displayed in the Title Bar
3. Select the Office Button 🔘 choose 🖨 Print ▸
4. The Print dialog box appears

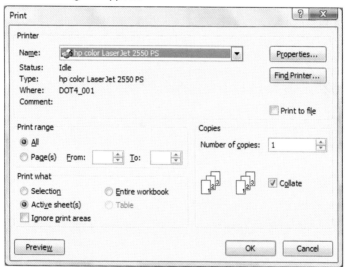

Figure 84

5. Choose Acti<u>v</u>e sheet(s)
6. Select ⌊ Previe<u>w</u> ⌋
7. Press 🔳 Next Page and 🔳 Previous Page to display the workbook
8. Click

Exercise 6: - Working with Multiple Sheets

1. Click on the Office Button select [New], choose [Blank Workbook]

2. Select [Create]

3. Rename four worksheets Qtr 1, Qtr 2, Qtr 3, Qtr 4

4. Group Sheets Qtr 1 to Qtr 4

5. Create the information below

	A	B	C	D	E	F
1		North	South	East	West	Total
2	Company 1					£0
3	Company 2					£0
4	Company 3					£0
5	Company 4					£0
6						
7	Total	£0	£0	£0	£0	

6. Format cells B2:F5 to Currency

7. Format B7:E7 to Currency

8. Use AutoSum to create the totals

9. Ungroup all the sheets

10. Select the sheet named Qtr 1

11. Create a copy of Qtr 1, rename the sheet Consolidation

12. In Qtr 1 type the following data

	A	B	C	D	E	F
1		North	South	East	West	Total
2	Company 1	£14,000	£86,000	£74,000	£89,000	£263,000
3	Company 2	£73,000	£89,000	£55,000	£23,000	£240,000
4	Company 3	£46,000	£29,000	£67,000	£15,000	£157,000
5	Company 4	£8,000	£43,000	£23,000	£18,000	£92,000
6						
7	Total	£141,000	£247,000	£219,000	£145,000	

13. In Qtr 2 type the following data

	A	B	C	D	E	F
1		North	South	East	West	Total
2	Company 1	£14,000	£7,000	£21,000	£20,000	£62,000
3	Company 2	£23,000	£11,000	£12,000	£10,000	£56,000
4	Company 3	£22,000	£46,000	£46,000	£46,000	£160,000
5	Company 4	£8,000	£8,000	£8,000	£8,000	£32,000
6						
7	Total	£67,000	£72,000	£87,000	£84,000	

14. In Qtr 3 type the following data

	A	B	C	D	E	F
1		North	South	East	West	Total
2	Company 1	£120,000	£86,000	£43,000	£28,000	£277,000
3	Company 2	£23,000	£132,000	£54,000	£45,000	£254,000
4	Company 3	£46,000	£120,000	£12,000	£33,000	£211,000
5	Company 4	£32,000	£8,000	£8,000	£8,000	£56,000
6						
7	Total	£221,000	£346,000	£117,000	£114,000	

15. Type the following data for Qtr 4

	A	B	C	D	E	F
1		North	South	East	West	Total
2	Company 1	£14,000	£14,000	£76,000	£14,000	£118,000
3	Company 2	£23,000	£122,000	£23,000	£23,000	£191,000
4	Company 3	£46,000	£18,000	£32,000	£63,000	£159,000
5	Company 4	£38,000	£12,000	£56,000	£83,000	£189,000
6						
7	Total	£121,000	£166,000	£187,000	£183,000	

16. Save the workbook as Working with Multiple Sheets

Creating 3 Dimensional Formula

To analyse data in the same cell or range of cells on multiple worksheets, it is possible to create a 3D formula.

1. Open the workbook Working with Multiple Sheets

2. Select the Consolidation worksheet and click on cell B2

3. To create a 3D formula Type =sum(

4. Click on worksheet Quarter 1

5. Hold the Shift key down, select worksheet Quarter 4

6. Select cell B2

7. The formula is displayed in the formula bar   =sum('Qtr1:Qtr4'!B2)

8. Click on the blue tick ✔ to confirm the formula

9. The result is displayed in cell B2 in the Consolidation Worksheet

10. Use the black cross fill handle to drag down to cell E5

11. The formula has added up the data in cell B2 in each quarter

12. Save to update the workbook

Note: **If a worksheet is moved or inserted into a workbook that contains a 3D formula, the formula incorporates the figures in the results of the formula. The opposite is true if a sheet was part of a 3D formula and the sheet was moved or deleted.**

Window Panes

Excel can freeze a column that will enable the heading rows to be seen at all times as you scroll across a worksheet.

Freeze Left Pane

1. Open the workbook Working with Multiple Sheets
2. Choose the worksheet named Quarter 4
3. Select cell B2
4. Click on [View], select [Freeze Panes ▾] from the Window Group
5. The following menu appears

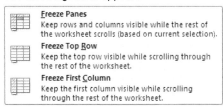

Freeze Panes
Keep rows and columns visible while the rest of the worksheet scrolls (based on current selection).

Freeze Top Row
Keep the top row visible while scrolling through the rest of the worksheet.

Freeze First Column
Keep the first column visible while scrolling through the rest of the worksheet.

Figure 85

6. Select Freeze Panes
7. Black indicator lines appear both to the left and above cell B2
8. Using the [→] key move along the row
9. The heading rows are visible as you move to cell Z2
10. To move back a cell at a time use the [←] key
11. Freeze panes ensures both column and row headings are visible
12. To unfreeze panes
13. Choose [Freeze Panes ▾], select **Unfreeze Panes** Unlock all rows and columns to scroll through the entire worksheet.

Note: Using Freeze Panes does not change or affect the printing of a worksheet.

To Freeze the Top Row

1. Select cell A2, the row below the Column Headings

2. Click on ⌐View⌐, select 🔲 Freeze Panes ▾ from the Window Group

3. The following menu appears

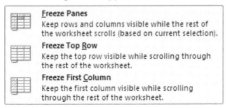

Figure 86

4. Select Freeze Top Row

5. A horizontal freeze pane line appears

6. Use the ⬇ to go to cell A75, all the column headings remain

7. Unfreeze the pane

Splitting a Window View

Splitting a window enables a user to view different areas of a large worksheet at the same time. The screen can be split into four different sections.

1. Click in cell B2

2. Select ⌐View⌐, choose ⌐Split from the Window Group

3. The screen splits into four sections

4. To move a split window

5. Move the mouse pointer ᐟᐠ over the split line

6. Press and hold down the left ᐟᗝ button, drag to the required position

7. To remove the split screen select ⌐Split

Saving Workbooks in Different Formats

There are occasions when a workbook needs to be saved in a different format, for example if a file needs to be saved in an earlier version format, Excel 97-2003.

1. Click on the Office Button 🔘 , choose 💾 Save As

2. Alternatively press F12 on the keyboard

3. The Save As dialog box appears

4. In the File name area type Expenses

5. In the Save as type box click on the downward pointing arrow

6. Select Excel 97-2003 workbook, click Save

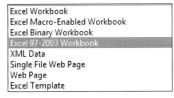

Figure 87

Working with Different Chart Types

Using different charts means that information can be easily understood by evaluating data and making it more interesting to read, charts can be used to help analyse and compare data.

Creating a 3-D Bar Stacked Chart

1. Create the following information below

	A	B	C	D	E	F
1		July	August	September	October	Total
2	**Resort A**	£23,400	£18,200	£20,421	£18,876	£80,897
3	**Resort B**	£13,275	£16,320	£20,745	£20,486	£70,826
4	**Resort C**	£44,739	£46,100	£32,400	£30,200	£153,439

Figure 88

2. Save the worksheet as Working with Charts

3. Highlight cells A1:D4, select Insert

4. Choose from the Charts Grouping

5. The charts menu appears, select Stacked Bar in 3-D

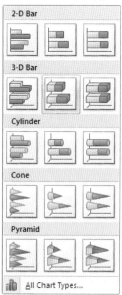

Figure 89

6. Click on from the Data Grouping

7. The layout of the Horizontal and Vertical axis changes

8. The selected area for the chart is displayed on the worksheet

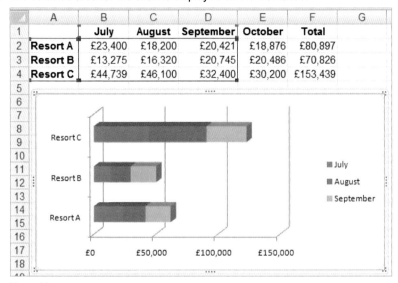

	A	B	C	D	E	F	G
1		July	August	September	October	Total	
2	Resort A	£23,400	£18,200	£20,421	£18,876	£80,897	
3	Resort B	£13,275	£16,320	£20,745	£20,486	£70,826	
4	Resort C	£44,739	£46,100	£32,400	£30,200	£153,439	

Figure 90

Customising a Chart

To remove or update data in the chart.

1. Click in the cell where information is to be removed or updated

2. Type in the changes, the chart is updated automatically

3. To add data to the chart

4. Click with the left ⌒ button in the chart area to activate the chart tools

5. Choose   Design , select the Chart Layouts Grouping

6. Use the downward pointing arrow ⤓ to expand the menu box

7. Choose Layout 7

Figure 91

8. Click on the Horizontal Axis Title, type Sales

9. Click on the Vertical Axis Title, type Location

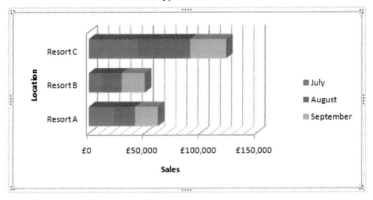

Figure 92

Adding New Data to a Chart

1. Click anywhere in the chart with the right 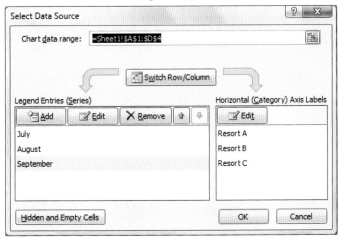 button

2. Choose ⊞ Select Data... from the menu

3. The Select Data Source dialog box appears

Figure 93

4. Click ⊞ Add , the Edit Series dialog box appears

Figure 94

5. Press the Series Name icon 🔢, select October

6. Click 🔲 to return to the Edit Series dialog box

7. Click on the Series Value icon 🔢, highlight cells E2 to E4

8. Click 🔲 to return to the Edit Series dialog box

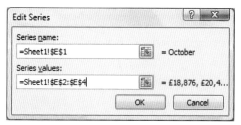

Figure 95

9. Press 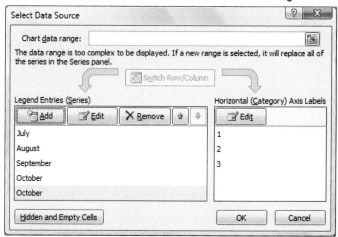 OK to return to the Select Data Source dialog box

Figure 96

10. Press OK to return to the updated chart

To Change the Type of Chart

1. Click in the chart, select `Design`, choose

2. Choose the chart type 100% Stacked Horizontal Cylinder

3. Press `OK`

4. To change the style of chart, select `Design`

5. Choose Chart Style 15

6. The chart is updated automatically

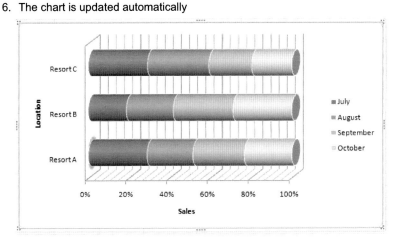

Figure 97

7. To remove the minor gridlines, click anywhere on the chart

8. Move the mouse pointer 🔍 over one of the minor gridlines

9. The following prompt appears `Horizontal (Value) Axis Minor Gridlines`

10. Click with the left 🖱 button to select the minor gridlines

11. Press the Delete key

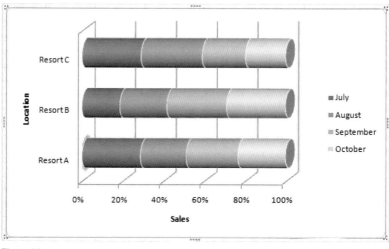

Figure 98

12. To change the background colour of the chart

13. Move the mouse pointer ⟨⟩ onto the back wall of the chart, | Back Wall | appears

14. Click with the left 🖱 button, blue circles ○ appear around the selected area

15. Click with the right 🖱 button, select | 🖳 Format Walls... |

16. Select | ⊙ Gradient fill |

17. Choose the background colour using the downward arrow | Color: 🖌 ▾ |

18. Press | Close |

19. To change the colour of the floor

20. Move the mouse pointer onto the floor area, | Floor | appears on the chart

21. Click with the right 🖱 button, select | 🖳 Format Floor... |

22. Select | ⊙ Solid fill |, choose the background colour | Color: 🖌 ▾ |

23. Select | Close |

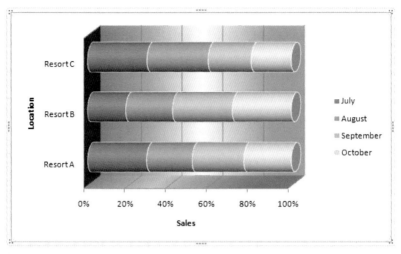

Figure 99

Adding Data Labels

1. Move the mouse pointer ⌖ over the October Series in the chart

2. Click with the right 🖱 button, select [Add Data Labels]

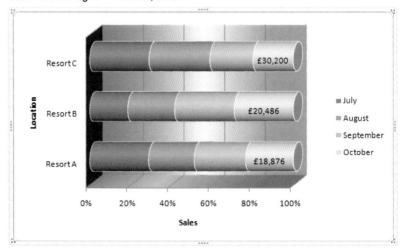

Figure 100

3. To format the data labels

4. Click with the right ⬚ button over the area, choose 📋 Format Data Labels...

5. The Format Data Labels dialog box appears

Figure 101

6. Select ☑ Series Name from the Label Options, press [Close]

7. October appears as the Data Label

Adding a Title to the Chart

1. Select the chart to display the Chart Tools

2. Choose [Layout], [Chart Title ▾], [Above Chart / Display Title at top of chart area and resize chart]

3. Type Customising Charts, press [Enter]

Changing the Chart using a 3-D Rotation

1. Move the mouse pointer over the back wall of the chart

2. Press the right button on the wall of the chart

3. Select [3-D Rotation...] , the Format Chart Area dialog box appears

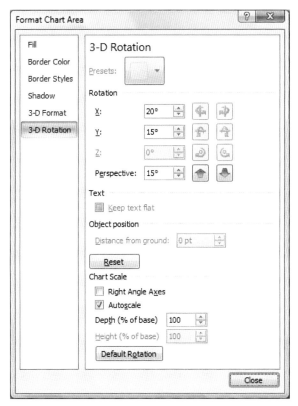

Figure 102

4. Change the Rotation as required

5. Ensure Right Angle Axes is **not** selected

6. Click [Close] to return to the chart

To Change the Type of Chart

1. Select Design , Change Chart Type

2. The Change Chart Type dialog box appears

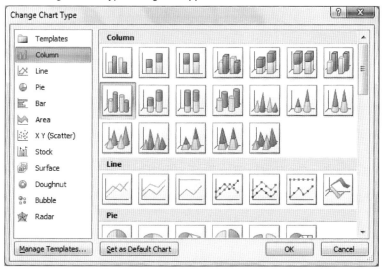

Figure 103

3. Select the chart type required, press OK

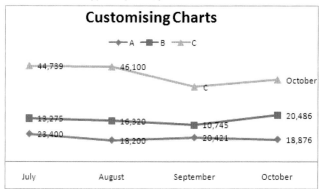

Figure 104

Interpreting Data in Charts

Charts can show the same data but in different formats allowing data to be interpreted in different ways.

1. Open the workbook Working with Charts

2. Click with the right 🖱 button inside the chart area

3. Choose Change Chart Type, select Line , Stacked line with Markers

4. Press OK

To Save a Chart as a Template

1. Click inside the chart area, the Chart Tools Tab appears

2. Select Save As Template, the Save Chart Template dialog box appears

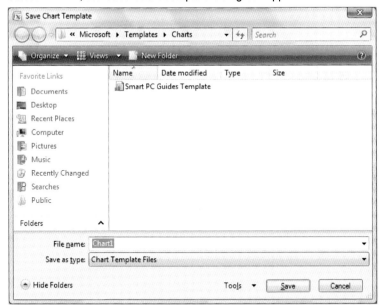

Figure 105

3. Create a name for the Chart Template and a description

4. Press Save

Vertical and Horizontal Lookup Functions

Lookup functions are useful to locate data in a selected table, database or list. Vertical Lookup (VLOOKUP) searches for a value in the left most column of a table and then returns a value in the same row from the selected column in the table, database or list. Horizontal Lookup (HLOOKUP) searches for a value in the top row of the table, database or list and returns a value in the same column from the selected row.

Vertical Lookup

1. Select a new worksheet, generate the following information

	A	B	C	D	E
1		Sales			
2	Name	2003	2004	2005	2006
3	Roger Ainsworth	£26,000	£26,950	£27,360	£27,750
4	Derek Bowen	£25,958	£26,925	£27,275	£27,800
5	Rachel James	£27,200	£26,970	£26,575	£27,100
6	Jeff Robson	£25,300	£26,100	£26,900	£27,000
7	Andy Scott	£26,000	£26,750	£27,150	£27,250
8	Burt Thomson	£27,900	£28,360	£28,956	£28,755
9	Lesley Turnbull	£25,320	£25,950	£26,300	£26,900
10	Donna Varney	£26,970	£27,110	£27,150	£27,390
11	Daniel Williams	£27,500	£26,100	£27,350	£27,735

Figure 106

2. Create the tabled information below to use in the vlookup formula

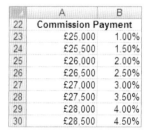

	A	B
22	Commission Payment	
23	£25,000	1.00%
24	£25,500	1.50%
25	£26,000	2.00%
26	£26,500	2.50%
27	£27,000	3.00%
28	£27,500	3.50%
29	£28,000	4.00%
30	£28,500	4.50%

Figure 107

3. Highlight cells A23:B30

4. Select Formulas

5. Choose Define Name from the Defined Names Grouping

6. The New Name dialog box appears

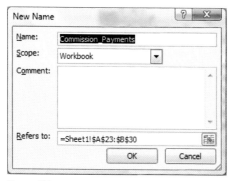

Figure 108

7. Type Commission_Payments in the **N**ame box

8. Click

9. Create the following information in cells A16 and A18

	A	B	C	D	E
16	Roger Ainsworth				
17					
18	Donna Varney				
19					

Figure 109

10. To create a vlookup formula, for quarterly commission payments as a %

11. Click in cell B16

12. Type **=vlookup(B3,Commission_Payments,2)**, press Enter

Note: **B4 in the formula represents Roger Ainsworth's Sales volume for the year 2000, Commission_Payments represents the named area used in the formula and the number 2 instructs the formula to look at the information in column 2.**

13. The result is 2% in cell B16

14. Click in cell B16, use the black fill handle to drag to E16

15. Format the cells into a percentage format

16. To calculate the formula as a £ value

17. Select cell B17 type =B3*B16 to calculate the amount of commission

18. This represents 26000 multiplied by 2%

19. Drag the relative formula to cell E17

20. Follow the steps to complete the information for Donna Varney

21. The results are outlined below

	A	B	C	D	E
16	Roger Ainsworth	2.00%	2.50%	3.00%	3.50%
17		£520.00	£673.75	£820.80	£971.25
18	Donna Varney	2.50%	3.00%	3.00%	3.00%
19		£674.25	£813.30	£814.50	£821.70

Figure 110

Using Horizontal Lookup

The formula for horizontal lookup is, select the column, select the table, select the row.

	A	B	C	D	E	F	G	H
1	Name	January	February	March	April	May	June	Totals
2	Goods In	£5,890.00	£4,671.00	£5,891.00	£4,998.00	£3,297.00	£3,789.00	£28,536.00
3	Sewing	£7,902.00	£7,857.00	£7,985.00	£6,342.00	£6,876.00	£7,203.00	£44,165.00
4	Tooling	£9,230.00	£7,350.00	£6,892.00	£5,890.00	£6,003.00	£5,907.00	£41,272.00
5	Spraying	£9,890.00	£7,750.00	£5,999.00	£6,002.00	£7,090.00	£6,325.00	£43,056.00
6	Maintenance	£11,009.00	£12,340.00	£15,700.00	£11,786.00	£10,906.00	£10,870.00	£72,611.00
7	Despatch	£14,560.00	£16,900.00	£15,650.00	£14,340.00	£14,980.00	£16,987.00	£93,417.00
8	Material	£15,900.00	£16,723.00	£17,230.00	£16,800.00	£15,236.00	£14,009.00	£95,898.00
9	Export	£17,340.00	£17,551.00	£17,340.00	£16,996.00	£18,000.00	£17,909.00	£105,136.00
10	Totals	£91,721.00	£91,142.00	£92,687.00	£83,154.00	£82,388.00	£82,999.00	

Figure 111

1. Open a new workbook, create the above table

2. Format the cells as shown

3. Highlight cells A1 to H10, select Formulas

4. Choose Define Name from the Defined Names Grouping

5. The New Name dialog box appears

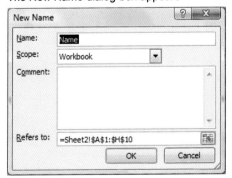

Figure 112

6. Type Production in the Name box, click OK

7. Using hlookup create a table that displays

    a. The monthly costs for Goods In for the months of January and May

    b. The results for January and May Goods In are £5,890 and £3,297

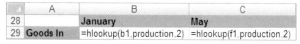

A	B	C
28	January	May
29 Goods In	=hlookup(b1,production,2)	=hlookup(f1,production,2)

Figure 113

8. Save the workbook as Using Horizontal Lookup

Note: Unlike vlookup, hlookup formulas are created individually. Displayed above is the result for January Goods In & May Goods In, the word "production" relates to the defined area A1:H10.

Exercise 7: - Using Horizontal Lookup

1. Open the workbook Using Horizontal Lookup

2. Using hlookup update the table to include

   a. The monthly costs for Despatch and Export for the months of January and May

   b. The Total costs for Goods In, Despatch and Export

	A	B	C	D
28		January	May	Totals
29	Goods In	£5,890.00	£3,297.00	
30	Despatch			
31	Export			

3. Save the workbook

Working with Comments

Excel allows you to insert comments to a cell that can easily be viewed or printed.

Insert Comments

1. Open an existing workbook, click in a cell

2. Select  , choose

3. A comments box appears

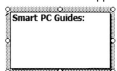

Figure 114

4. Alternatively press Shift F2 to display the comments box

5. Type the required text

6. Click outside the comment to deselect

7. A red 🗨 marker appears in the cell containing the comment

To View a Comment

1. Move the cursor into the cell containing the comment

2. The comments box appears

3. To deselect, move the cursor outside the cell

4. Alternatively press F5, the Go To dialog box appears

Figure 115

5. Select [Special...]

6. The Go To Special dialog box appears

Figure 116

7. Select **C**omments, click [OK]

8. All the cells containing comments are highlighted

9. To view any comment move the mouse pointer ⇖ over the highlighted cell

Edit a Comment

1. Select [Review], click in the cell that contains a comment, choose Edit Comment

2. Amend the comment, click back in the cell with the edited comment

3. The edited comment is displayed

To Delete a Comment

1. Select [Review], choose Delete

2. The comment is deleted from the cell

To Show All Comments in a Worksheet

1. To display all the comments, choose Show All Comments

2. To hide all the comments, reselect Show All Comments

To Show/Hide Comments in a Selected Cell

1. Click on a cell that contains a comment

2. Choose Show/Hide Comment , the comment is displayed

3. To hide the comment, reselect Show/Hide Comment

To Move a Comments Box

1. Click on Show All Comments

2. Position the cursor over the edge of the comments box

3. Click with the left button, drag to the new location

To Adjust the Size of the Comments Box

1. Select Show All Comments

2. Position the cursor over the edge of the comments box

3. Press the left button, using the resizing handles drag to the new size

To Print Comments

1. Select Page Layout , choose the Page Setup Grouping

2. Click with the left button on the dialog box launcher

3. The Page Setup dialog box appears

4. Select the Sheet Tab

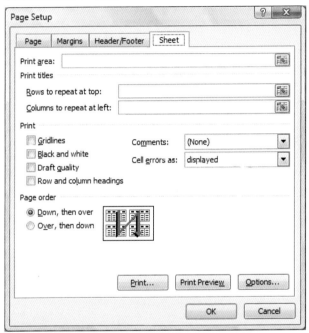

Figure 117

5. In the Comments area, select As displayed on sheet or At end of sheet

6. Press Print Preview to display the comments on the worksheet

7. Choose Next Page to display the comments throughout the worksheet

8. Press Print or Close Print Preview to return to the worksheet

Password Protection

Excel provides several ways to restrict access to a workbook or prevent changes to the structure of a workbook, such as moving, deleting or adding sheets by assigning a password.

IMPORTANT INFORMATION ABOUT YOUR PASWORD - WRITE IT DOWN AND KEEP IT SAFE. **If you lose the password, you cannot open or gain access to the data in the password protected workbook**.

Protecting a Workbook

1. Open a workbook

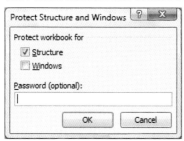

2. Click on Review , select Protect Workbook from the Changes Group
3. The Protect Structure and Windows dialog box appears

Figure 118

4. Place a tick ☑ in the **S**tructure box to protect the structure of the workbook
5. Passwords are case sensitive
6. In the **P**assword (optional) box type in a password of your choice
7. Press OK

Confirm Password

Reenter password to proceed.

Caution: If you lose or forget the password, it cannot be recovered. It is advisable to keep a list of passwords and their corresponding workbook and sheet names in a safe place. (Remember that passwords are case-sensitive.)

OK   Cancel

Figure 119

8. Re-enter the password, click [OK], save the workbook

9. To alter the structure of the workbook, for example adding a new worksheet

10. Double click with the left 🖱 button on sheet 1

11. The following dialog box appears

Figure 120

12. Click [OK]

To Change a Password

1. Open a workbook

2. Select the Office Button 🔵 , choose  Save As ▸

3. Click [Tools ▼] from the bottom of the Save As dialog box

4. Choose General Options...

5. The General Options dialog box appears

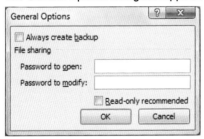

Figure 121

6. Select Password to **m**odify, type in the new password

7. Click [OK]

8. The Confirm Password dialog box appears

9. Retype the password

Figure 122

10. Press save the workbook

To Remove a Password

1. Open a workbook, click on Review

2. Select Unprotect Workbook from the Changes Group

3. The Unprotect Workbook dialog appears

Figure 123

4. Type in the password to be deleted, press OK

5. Save the workbook

Protecting a Sheet

1. Open a workbook, click on

2. Select  from the Changes Group

3. The Protect Sheet dialog box appears

Figure 124

4. Click OK

5. Alternatively type a password, Re-enter password again

6. Press OK

Protecting a Range

	A	B	C	D	E	F	G	H
1	Name	January	February	March	April	May	June	Totals
2	Goods In	£5,890.00	£4,671.00	£5,891.00	£4,998.00	£3,297.00	£3,789.00	£28,536.00
3	Sewing	£7,902.00	£7,857.00	£7,985.00	£6,342.00	£6,876.00	£7,203.00	£44,165.00
4	Tooling	£9,230.00	£7,350.00	£6,892.00	£5,890.00	£6,003.00	£5,907.00	£41,272.00
5	Spraying	£9,890.00	£7,750.00	£5,999.00	£6,002.00	£7,090.00	£6,325.00	£43,056.00
6	Maintenance	£11,009.00	£12,340.00	£15,700.00	£11,786.00	£10,906.00	£10,870.00	£72,611.00
7	Despatch	£14,560.00	£16,900.00	£15,650.00	£14,340.00	£14,980.00	£16,987.00	£93,417.00
8	Material	£15,900.00	£16,723.00	£17,230.00	£16,800.00	£15,236.00	£14,009.00	£95,898.00
9	Export	£17,340.00	£17,551.00	£17,340.00	£16,996.00	£18,000.00	£17,909.00	£105,136.00
10	Totals	£91,721.00	£91,142.00	£92,687.00	£83,154.00	£82,388.00	£82,999.00	

Figure 125

1. Open the workbook Using Horizontal Lookup

2. Click on Review

3. Select Allow Users to Edit Ranges from the Change Grouping

4. The Allow Users to Edit Ranges dialog box appears

Figure 126

5. Select New..., the New Range dialog box appears

Figure 127

6. Type January in the Title area

7. Select  in the refer to cells area

8. Select cells B2:B10, click to confirm the range

9. In the Range password area, type January

10. Click OK, re-enter the password, press OK

Figure 128

11. Select Protect Sheet..., click OK

12. Save the worksheet

13. Click in cell F5, try to change the data in this cell

14. The following prompt appears

Figure 129

15. Alternatively double click in cell B8, the following dialog box appears

Figure 130

16. Enter January in the password area, click [OK]

17. Amendments to the selected range can now be made

18. Save and close the workbook

Filtering Data

Sorting and filtering large amounts of data within a worksheet using the AutoFilter and Advanced Filter is a useful way of displaying data as a sub-section view.

Sorting and Filtering Data

	A	B	C	D	E	F	G	H
1	Location	Section	Surname	First Name	DOB	Start Date	Job Title	Salary
2	Leeds	HR	Roberts	Samuel	09/03/1954	27/03/1976	HR Officer	£33,276
3	Newark	Logistics	Gillespie	Nicola	08/01/1957	08/08/1989	Manager	£18,230
4	Leicester	Payroll	Davies	Terry	08/02/1958	02/01/1988	Payroll Clerk	£13,250
5	Leicester	Logistics	Collins	laura	16/06/1963	11/10/2000	Traffic Admin	£16,570
6	Leeds	HR	Lesley	David	14/07/1963	12/12/1985	HR Officer	£32,950
7	Barnsley	Accounts	Gilliam	Diana	13/10/1967	15/07/1990	Cost Clerk	£11,357
8	Derby	HR	Payne	Barry	21/10/1970	07/12/2000	HR Manager	£29,950
9	Grantham	Accounts	Andrews	Colin	26/03/1972	01/01/1992	Clerk	£13,760
10	Rotherham	Training	Rogers	Rachel	16/01/1976	01/10/1991	Training Manager	£27,950
11	Derby	IT	Cobb	Jane	05/05/1976	29/09/1996	Consultant	£27,350
12	Leeds	Buying	Smith	Melanie	27/11/1981	19/08/2001	Buying Clerk	£8,100
13	Sheffield	Marketing	Hopkins	James	08/04/1983	03/06/2003	Clerk	£15,600
14	Grantham	Buying	Buckley	Christopher	17/07/1984	17/07/1984	Buyer	£25,250
15	Barnsley	Payroll	Brooks	Thomas	12/08/1984	20/07/2000	Payroll Clerk	£8,950
16	Sheffield	IT	Michael	Phillip	10/07/1985	01/12/2002	Consultant	£27,350
17	Rotherham	IT	Bassett	Michael	09/07/1986	01/12/2002	Consultant	£30,205
18	Mansfield	Customer Care	Vale	Andrew	13/11/1987	19/04/2001	Care Clerk	£10,590

Figure 131

1. Open a blank new workbook, create the above data within a worksheet

2. Save the workbook as Sorting and Filtering Data

3. Click in cell A6, select [Home]

4. Choose [Sort & Filter] from the Editing Grouping, select

5. The worksheet is updated automatically

Filtering Data using Several Criteria

To generate a sort using the criteria Section in ascending order, Job Title in ascending order and Salary in descending order

1. Click in a cell that contains data, choose Home

2. Select Filter▾ from the Editing Grouping

3. Choose ⊞ Custom Sort... , the Sort dialog box appears

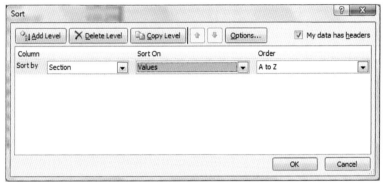

Figure 132

4. In the Sort by box, select Section and Order A to Z, select ⌂▴|Add Level

5. In the Then by box, select Job Title and Order A to Z, select ⌂▴|Add Level

6. In the Then by box select, Salary and Order Smallest to Largest

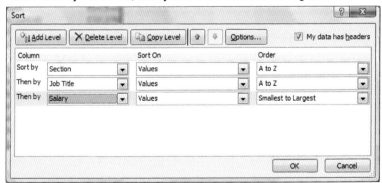

Figure 133

7. Click   OK

Using the Filter Icon

1. Click on a cell containing the list of data, select  Home

2. Choose Sort & Filter ▼ from the Editing Grouping, select Y= Filter

3. In the headings a downward arrow indicates the filtering option

4. Click on the arrow in the heading Section ▼

5. Select Buying, IT and Marketing, click OK

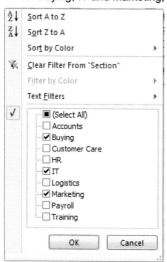

Figure 134

6. The filter icon appears when a filter is applied in the Column Heading

7. Members of staff in the Buying, IT and Marketing sections are displayed

	A	B	C	D	E	F	G	H
1	Location ▼	Section ▼	Surnam ▼	First Name ▼	DOB ▼	Start Date ▼	Job Title ▼	Salary ▼
4	Grantham	Buying	Buckley	Christopher	17/07/1984	17/07/1984	Buyer	£25,250
5	Leeds	Buying	Smith	Melanie	27/11/1981	19/08/2001	Buying Clerk	£8,100
10	Derby	IT	Cobb	Jane	05/05/1976	29/09/1996	Consultant	£27,350
11	Sheffield	IT	Michael	Phillip	10/07/1985	01/12/2002	Consultant	£27,350
12	Rotherham	IT	Bassett	Michael	09/07/1986	01/12/2002	Consultant	£30,205
15	Sheffield	Marketing	Hopkins	James	08/04/1983	03/06/2003	Clerk	£15,600

Figure 135

8. Row numbers that match the criteria change to blue

9. To remove the filter click on the filter icon

10. Choose 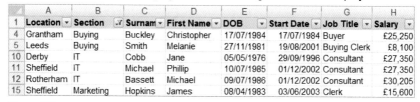 ☑ (Select All) press OK

Creating a Custom Filter

1. Click on the arrow in the heading **Salary** ▾

2. Select | Number Filters ▶ |, | Equals... |

3. The Custom AutoFilter dialog box appears, complete the Custom AutoFilter

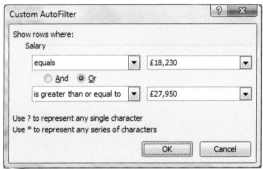

Figure 136

4. Click | OK |, the data is displayed as follows

	A	B	C	D	E	F	G	H
1	Location ▾	Section ▾	Surname ▾	First Name ▾	DOB ▾	Start Date ▾	Job Title ▾	Salary ⟱
7	Derby	HR	Payne	Barry	21/10/1970	07/12/2000	HR Manager	£29,950
8	Leeds	HR	Lesley	David	14/07/1963	12/12/1985	HR Officer	£32,950
9	Leeds	HR	Roberts	Samuel	09/03/1954	27/03/1976	HR Officer	£33,276
12	Rotherham	IT	Bassett	Michael	09/07/1986	01/12/2002	Consultant	£30,205
13	Newark	Logistics	Gillespie	Nicola	08/01/1957	08/08/1989	Manager	£18,230
18	Rotherham	Training	Rogers	Rachel	16/01/1976	01/10/1991	Training Manager	£27,950

Figure 137

5. Create a custom filter of your choice based upon the salary data

Advanced Filter

The Advanced Filter is used to create more complex criteria to be filtered.

1. Using the workbook Sorting and Filtering Data

2. Click in a blank cell beneath the main data

3. Type or copy the headings for the advanced filter as shown below

Location	Salary	Salary
Rotherham	>=15000	
Leeds	>=18000	<=34000

Figure 138

4. In this instance the advanced filter has been asked to locate staff with salaries greater than or equal to £15,000 in Rotherham and salaries greater than or equal to £18,000 but less than or equal to £34,000 in Leeds

5. Click anywhere in the original data

6. Sort the location field into alphabetical order

7. Select ⌷ Data ⌷, choose ⌷ Advanced ⌷ from the Sort & Filter Grouping

8. The Advanced Filter dialog box appears

Figure 139

9. A dotted line appears around the original data

10. In this example, click with the left ⌷ button to Copy to another location

11. Press ⌷ Tab ⌷, the original data is highlighted in the List range area

12. Select ⌷ Tab ⌷ to move to the Criteria range

13. Click the ⌷ icon to select the advanced criteria including the headings

14. Click the ⌷ icon to return to the Advanced Filter dialog box

15. Press ⌷ Tab ⌷ to move to Copy to

16. Click in cell A30, choose ⌷ OK ⌷

17. The results are shown below

30	Location	Section	Surname	First Name	DOB	Start Date	Job Title	Salary
31	Leeds	HR	Lesley	David	14/07/1963	12/12/1985	HR Officer	£32,950
32	Leeds	HR	Roberts	Samuel	09/03/1954	27/03/1976	HR Officer	£33,276
33	Rotherham	IT	Bassett	Michael	09/07/1986	01/12/2002	Consultant	£30,205
34	Rotherham	Training	Rogers	Rachel	16/01/1976	01/10/1991	Training Manager	£27,950

Figure 140

Exercise 8: - Using the Advanced Filter

1. Open the workbook Sorting and Filtering Data
2. Set the criteria to find staff based in Barnsley and Leicester
3. Copy the advanced filter to another location
4. The result shows four people that match the criteria
5. Return to the original data
6. Using the advanced filter, define the criteria to find Nicola Gillespie and Colin Andrews
7. The results show the data on Nicola Gillespie and Colin Andrews
8. Return to the original data
9. Save the workbook

Using the Subtotals Feature

1. Open the workbook Sorting and Filtering Data

2. Sort the Section area into alphabetical order

3. Select Data, choose Subtotal from the Outline Grouping

4. The Subtotal dialog box appears

5. Select the following criteria

Figure 141

6. Click OK, the results are shown below

Figure 142

7. There are 3 outline icons to the left of Column A 1 2 3

8. Select 1 to display the grand total

9. Select 2 to display the Section Totals

10. Select 3 to display all the criteria

Removing Subtotals

1. Click in the original data

2. Select , choose from the Outline Grouping, select

Section 3: Expert Level Objectives

- Creating Range Names

- Auditing a Worksheet

- Using Watch Window

- Strings and Text Functions

- Logical Functions

- Outlining a Worksheet

- Data Consolidation

- Templates

- Scenario Manager

- Custom Views

- PivotTables

- Macros

- Quick Access Toolbar

- Excel File Formats

- Shortcut Keys

**Note: If you are working in Windows XP instead of Windows Vista, dialog
        boxes may look different but function in a similar way.**

Range Names

When working in Excel a cell or block of cells can be defined using meaningful names, for example =sum(A2:D2) can be defined as =Sum(Leeds:Leicester). Names can be applied to formulas.

Advantages of Range Names

1. It is easier to remember a name rather than a cell reference
2. Formulas are easier to understand
3. When a name is redefined all formulas using the name are updated
4. Using Range Names makes navigation around a worksheet faster

Define a Range Name

1. Click with the left button in a cell or selected range of cells
2. Select   Formulas   , choose   Define Name ▾
3. The New Name dialog box appears

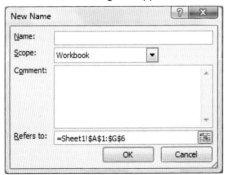

Figure 143

4. In the **N**ame box, define a specific name for the range of cells
5. In the **S**cope box select workbook or the sheet the range name refers to
6. In the C**o**mment box enter a descriptive comment
7. Click   OK
8. Click in any cell outside the selected range
9. Move the cursor to the Name Box area [▾ (fx] on the Formula Bar
10. Click on the downward pointing arrow ▾, select the newly defined name
11. The range is highlighted

Delete a Defined Name

1. Select | Formulas |, choose Name Manager or press Ctrl F3
2. The Name Manager dialog box appears
3. Click with the left 🖱 button on the name to be deleted, press | Delete |
4. Select | OK |
5. Choose | Close |

Creating a Range of Names

Using the 'create from selection' feature allows multiple names to be created in one instruction.

1. Create the following information

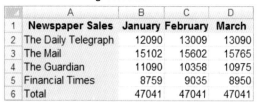

	A	B	C	D
1	**Newspaper Sales**	**January**	**February**	**March**
2	The Daily Telegraph	12090	13009	13090
3	The Mail	15102	15602	15765
4	The Guardian	11090	10358	10975
5	Financial Times	8759	9035	8950
6	Total	47041	47041	47041

Figure 144

2. Highlight cells A1:D5
3. Select | Formulas |, choose, 🔠 Create from Selection
4. The Create Names from Selection dialog box appears

Figure 145

5. Select Top row and Left Column, click | OK |
6. Move the cursor to the Name Box area on the Formula Bar
7. Click the downward pointing arrow ▾, select "The Mail", the data is highlighted

Using the Apply Names Feature

Using formulas in the selected area before names are applied means formula names are not displayed, in order for the formula to be displayed, a name has to be applied.

	A	B	C	D
1	**Newspaper Sales**	**January**	**February**	**March**
2	The Daily Telegraph	12090	13009	13090
3	The Mail	15102	15602	15765
4	The Guardian	11090	10358	10975
5	Financial Times	8759	9035	8950
6	Total	47041	47041	47041

Figure 146

1. Highlight cells A1:D6

2. Select  Formulas , click on the downward arrow on ⊞ Define Name ▾

3. Choose Apply Names... , the Apply Names dialog box appears

Figure 147

4. Choose OK , the names have been applied

5. Click in cell B6, C6 and D6, the names have been applied to the formulas

6. Select a empty cell, type =The_Mail January + The_Guardian January

7. Press Enter, the total for The Mail and The Guardian for January is displayed

8. Select cell E2, type =SUM(The_Daily_Telegraph)

9. Press Enter, the total for The Daily Telegraph is displayed

10. Select cell E3, type =The_Mail January + February + March

11. Press [Enter], the total for The Mail for January, February and March is displayed

12. Create the totals for The Guardian and the Financial Times

Delete a Range of Names

1. Select cells C1:C6

2. Choose [Home], select [Delete ▾]

3. If a total displays [#REF!] when data has been deleted, the total will need to be recalculated by deleting February from the formula

4. Save the workbook as Working with Names and Ranges

Displaying Range Names

To view an index of the range names applied in a worksheet.

1. Click in the empty cell H1 to display the information

2. Select [Formulas], choose [ƒ Use in Formula ▾], [Paste Names...]

3. The Paste Name dialog box appears

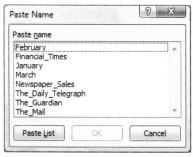

Figure 148

4. Select [Paste List], the applied names and references are displayed

February	=Sheet1!$C$2:$C$5
Financial_Times	=Sheet1!$B$5:$D$5
January	=Sheet1!$B$2:$B$5
March	=Sheet1!$D$2:$D$5
Newspaper_Sales	=Sheet1!$B$2:$D$5
The_Daily_Telegraph	=Sheet1!$B$2:$D$2
The_Guardian	=Sheet1!$B$4:$D$4
The_Mail	=Sheet1!$B$3:$D$3

Figure 149

Note: The list will not automatically update if new names are added.

Using the Auditing Functions

Excel allows formulas and results in a worksheet to be traced using the Formula Auditing Grouping.

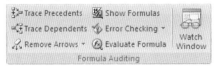

Figure 150

Using Trace Precedent and Dependent Features

1. Create the following worksheet

	A	B	C	D	E	F	G
1	Sales	January	February	March	April	May	Total
2							
3	Monday	11500	14000	11125	11765	15122	63512
4	Tuesday	12000	14001	13234	11000	13245	63480
5	Wednesday	14000	14002	12678	11200	19174	71054
6	Thursday	16000	14003	10976	11300	13328	65607
7	Friday	18000	14004	16740	11400	19884	80028
8	Saturday	20000	14005	10308	11500	19487	75300
9	Sunday	22000	14006	13444	11600	16029	77079
10							
11	Monthly Total	113500	98021	88505	79765	116269	

Figure 151

2. Select cell G3, click on the ⌘ Trace Precedents icon

3. Tracer arrows display the cells that provide data to the formula

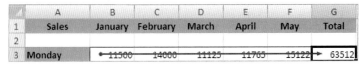

Figure 152

4. To remove the arrows click on the Remove Arrows icon

5. Select cell C6, click on Trace Dependents

	A	B	C	D	E	F	G
1	**Sales**	**January**	**February**	**March**	**April**	**May**	**Total**
2							
3	Monday	11500	14000	11125	11765	15122	63512
4	Tuesday	12000	14001	13234	11000	13245	63480
5	Wednesday	14000	14002	12678	11200	19174	71054
6	Thursday	16000	14003	10976	11300	13328	65607
7	Friday	18000	14004	16740	11400	19884	80028
8	Saturday	20000	14005	10308	11500	19487	75300
9	Sunday	22000	14006	13444	11600	16029	77079
10							
11	Monthly Total	113500	98021	88505	79765	116269	

Figure 153

6. Tracer arrows highlight the cells containing data to the formula

7. To remove the arrows click on [Remove Arrows ▾]

8. Save the Workbook as Using Auditing Functions

Using Trace Error Features

1. If an error occurs, select the cell containing the error message

2. Choose [Error Checking ▾]

3. The Error Checking dialog box appears, displaying the cell reference

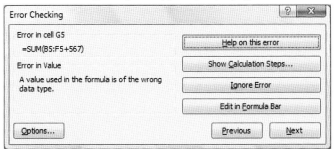

Figure 154

4. Choose [Next] to identify the type of error

5. Press [Edit in Formula Bar]

6. Amend the reference manually

7. Select the ✓ to accept the change, choose [Resume]

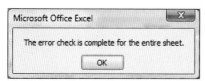

Figure 155

8. Click

Note: **The Trace Error Feature will display errors in any worksheet within an open workbook. If formulas are contained in another workbook that workbook needs to be opened to complete the full check.**

Using the Watch Window

The Watch Window feature allows the user to monitor the values of cells.

1. Open the workbook named Using Auditing Functions

2. Rename the worksheet as Monthly Sales Figures

3. Select from the Formula Auditing Grouping

4. The Watch Window dialog box appears

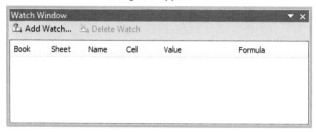

Figure 156

5. Highlight cells G3:G9, choose 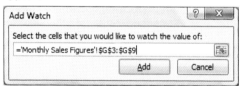, the Add Watch window appears

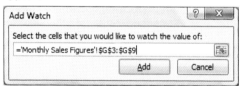

Figure 157

6. Click [Add], the highlighted cells appear in the Watch Window

Book	Sheet	Name	Cell	Value	Formula
Using Auditing Functions.xlsx	Monthly Sales Figures		G3	63512	=SUM(B3:F3)
Using Auditing Functions.xlsx	Monthly Sales Figures		G4	63480	=SUM(B4:F4)
Using Auditing Functions.xlsx	Monthly Sales Figures		G5	71054	=SUM(B5:F5)
Using Auditing Functions.xlsx	Monthly Sales Figures		G6	65607	=SUM(B6:F6)
Using Auditing Functions.xlsx	Monthly Sales Figures		G7	80028	=SUM(B7:F7)
Using Auditing Functions.xlsx	Monthly Sales Figures		G8	75300	=SUM(B8:F8)
Using Auditing Functions.xlsx	Monthly Sales Figures		G9	77079	=SUM(B9:F9)

Figure 158

7. Select cell B11, add the Monthly Total to the Watch Window

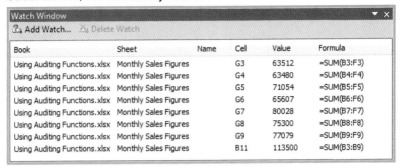

Figure 159

8. Add cells C11,D11,E11 and F11 to the Watch Window

9. To delete a Watch Window reference, select the item, choose

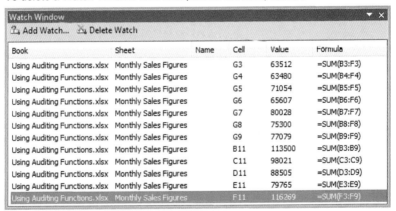

Figure 160

Items within the Watch Window

1. The Watch Window displays the name of the Workbook, Sheet, Cell, Value and Formula

2. The user can watch cells and their formulas even when out of view

3. To display formulas in another workbook, the workbook must be opened

4. A defined name for a formula is displayed in the ⎡ Name ⎤ area

5. To sort by value, select ⎡ Value ⎤

Strings and Text Functions

A string is a sequence of characters entered as a label in Excel. Labels used in formulas are String Values. Formulas that contain more than one string value are referred to as string expressions and must begin with an = (equal symbol). String expressions joined together are concatenated. The following example displays how concatenation works.

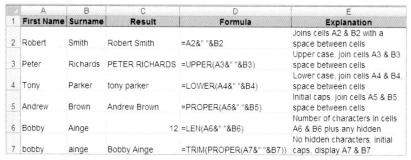

	A	B	C	D	E
1	**First Name**	**Surname**	**Result**	**Formula**	**Explanation**
2	Robert	Smith	Robert Smith	=A2&" "&B2	Joins cells A2 & B2 with a space between cells
3	Peter	Richards	PETER RICHARDS	=UPPER(A3&" "&B3)	Upper case, join cells A3 & B3, space between cells
4	Tony	Parker	tony parker	=LOWER(A4&" "&B4)	Lower case, join cells A4 & B4, space between cells
5	Andrew	Brown	Andrew Brown	=PROPER(A5&" "&B5)	Initial caps, join cells A5 & B5, space between cells
6	Bobby	Ainge		12 =LEN(A6&" "&B6)	Number of characters in cells A6 & B6 plus any hidden
7	bobby	ainge	Bobby Ainge	=TRIM(PROPER(A7&" "&B7))	No hidden characters, initial caps, display A7 & B7

Figure 161

Functions are organised by category, such as Text and Logical (whether an argument is true or false), an argument can be numbers, text, logical values, tables or functions. A function is made up of **Function_Name(argument1, argument2 …..)**, an argument is the information that a function uses to produce a **New Value** or perform an action.

Using the Function Wizard

The Function Wizard provides an easy guide to creating all formulas.

1. Click in a cell, choose

2. The Insert Function dialog box appears

3. In the Search for a function box type "Text in Upper Case", press [Go]

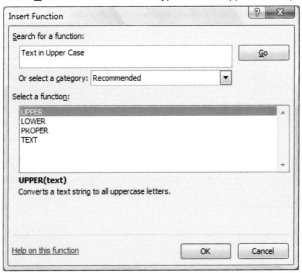

Figure 162

4. Click [OK], the Function Arguments dialog box appears

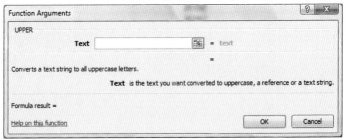

Figure 163

5. In the Text box type smart pc guides, click [OK]

6. The text appears in uppercase, the formula is =UPPER("smart pc guides")

Exercise 9: - Using the Function Wizard

1. Create the following table in a new worksheet

2. Using the Function Wizard and Quick Reference Formula

Department	Names	Quick Reference
Human Resources		Create in Uppercase
CreDit CONtroller	ANNe SparRow	Create in Propercase
PRoject OfFiceR	JUDY Crow	Create in Propercase
HR Clerk	HaRry Swift	Create in Uppercase
FinaNCe oFficer	JOHN starling	Create in Lowercase

3. Insert a column to display a copy of each working formula

4. The results from the exercise are displayed below

Department	Names
HUMAN RESOURCES	
Credit Controller	Anne Sparrow
Project Officer	Judy Crow
HR CLERK	HARRY SWIFT
finance officer	john starling

5. Save the worksheet Working with the Function Wizard

Search and Find Functions

The search function defined, as *Search* is not case sensitive and allows a character or text string to be located, whereas the find function *Find* can locate a character or text string but is case sensitive.

Working with Search and Find

The following table provides a brief example of how the search and find functions work. It is important to plan the formula; brackets are colour coded =(((()))) when opened brackets are applied equal amounts of closed brackets need be used.

	A	B	C	D
2	SMART GUIDES	6	=SEARCH(" ",A2)	Search & display number of characters to space in cell
3	SMART GUIDES	6	=FIND(" ",A3)	Find & display number of characters to space in cell
4	SMART GUIDES	12	=LEN(A4)	Display number of characters in cell A4
5	SMART GUIDES	6	=LEN(A5)-SEARCH(" ",A5)	Search & display number of characters after the space
6	SMART GUIDES	6	=LEN(A6)-FIND(" ",A6)	Find & display number of characters after the space
7	SMART GUIDES	GUIDES	=RIGHT(A7,LEN(A7)-SEARCH(" ",A7))	Search & display from the right number of characters
8	SMART GUIDES	GUIDES	=RIGHT(A8,LEN(A8)-FIND(" ",A7))	Find & display from the right characters after the space
9	SMART GUIDES	SMART	=LEFT(A9,SEARCH(" ",A9))	Search & display characters to the left of the space
10	SMART GUIDES	SMART	=LEFT(A10,FIND(" ",A10))	Find & display characters to the left of the space
11	SMART GUIDES	Smart	=PROPER(LEFT(A11,SEARCH(" ",A11)))	characters to the left of the space in initial caps
12	SMART GUIDES	Guides	=PROPER(RIGHT(A12,LEN(A12)-FIND(" ",A12)))	characters after the space in initial caps

Figure 164

Exercise 10: - Working with Search and Find

1. Open a new workbook
2. Type out your first name and surname in a cell of your choice
3. Showing working formulas, find the number of characters in the cell
4. Find the number of characters from the left of the space
5. Search and display in lowercase the characters to the right of the space
6. Search and display in uppercase the characters to the left of the space
7. Save the workbook as Search and Find

Logical Functions

The "**IF**" function allows users to construct and analyse a formula's validity performing an action that calculates whether a statement is TRUE or FALSE. Up to seven **IF** statements can be grouped together (Nested) to construct a more detailed result. To test a statement, Excel evaluates a logical equation returning the word TRUE if the formula statement is true or FALSE if the statement is false.

Description	Symbol Used
Equal to	=
Greater than	>
Less than	<
Not equal to	<>
Greater than or equal to	>=
Less than or equal to	<=

Figure 165

Using the IF Function

1. Open a new workbook, create the following information

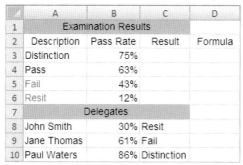

	A	B	C	D
1	Examination Results			
2	Description	Pass Rate	Result	Formula
3	Distinction	75%		
4	Pass	63%		
5	Fail	43%		
6	Resit	12%		
7	Delegates			
8	John Smith	30%	Resit	
9	Jane Thomas	61%	Fail	
10	Paul Waters	86%	Distinction	

Figure 166

2. Select cell C8, following the formula below, generate the results for the 3 delegates

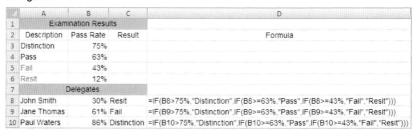

	A	B	C	D
1	Examination Results			
2	Description	Pass Rate	Result	Formula
3	Distinction	75%		
4	Pass	63%		
5	Fail	43%		
6	Resit	12%		
7	Delegates			
8	John Smith	30%	Resit	=IF(B8>75%,"Distinction",IF(B8>=63%,"Pass",IF(B8>=43%,"Fail","Resit")))
9	Jane Thomas	61%	Fail	=IF(B9>75%,"Distinction",IF(B9>=63%,"Pass",IF(B9>=43%,"Fail","Resit")))
10	Paul Waters	86%	Distinction	=IF(B10>75%,"Distinction",IF(B10>=63%,"Pass",IF(B10>=43%,"Fail","Resit")))

Figure 167

3. Save the workbook as Working with Nested Statements

Exercise 11: - Creating Nested Statements

1. Open a new workbook

2. Create a table displaying bank interest rates on a current account

3. Use the following rates

Rates	
2%	<=1000
3%	>2000
4%	>4345
5%	>6420

Note: **When using IF statements work from the HIGHEST VALUE downwards, make sure the percentage values are between inverted commas.**

4. Create IF Statements for the following amounts

Current Account (£)
2000
4500
6690
63

5. Save the workbook Working with Nested Statements

Using Outlining in Worksheets

Excel allows the user to create summary reports by using the Outline Function to show or hide data by grouping data by column or rows using Automatic Outline or Manual Outline.

Creating a Automatic Outline

1. Open a new workbook
2. Create the following information

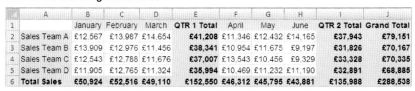

	A	B	C	D	E	F	G	H	I	J
1		January	February	March	QTR 1 Total	April	May	June	QTR 2 Total	Grand Total
2	Sales Team A	£12,567	£13,987	£14,654	£41,208	£11,346	£12,432	£14,165	£37,943	£79,151
3	Sales Team B	£13,909	£12,976	£11,456	£38,341	£10,954	£11,675	£9,197	£31,826	£70,167
4	Sales Team C	£12,543	£12,788	£11,676	£37,007	£13,543	£10,456	£9,329	£33,328	£70,335
5	Sales Team D	£11,905	£12,765	£11,324	£35,994	£10,469	£11,232	£11,190	£32,891	£68,885
6	Total Sales	£50,924	£52,516	£49,110	£152,550	£46,312	£45,795	£43,881	£135,988	£288,538

Figure 168

3. Click in the data to be outlined, Choose, Data, Group, Auto Outline

	A	B	C	D	E	F	G	H	I	J
1		January	February	March	QTR 1 Total	April	May	June	QTR 2 Total	Grand Total
2	Sales Team A	£12,567	£13,987	£14,654	£41,208	£11,346	£12,432	£14,165	£37,943	£79,151
3	Sales Team B	£13,909	£12,976	£11,456	£38,341	£10,954	£11,675	£9,197	£31,826	£70,167
4	Sales Team C	£12,543	£12,788	£11,676	£37,007	£13,543	£10,456	£9,329	£33,328	£70,335
5	Sales Team D	£11,905	£12,765	£11,324	£35,994	£10,469	£11,232	£11,190	£32,891	£68,885
6	Total Sales	£50,924	£52,516	£49,110	£152,550	£46,312	£45,795	£43,881	£135,988	£288,538

Figure 169

4. The horizontal outlines are displayed above the column
5. The vertical outlines are displayed to the left of the rows
6. In the horizontal area, choose 1 to view Grand Totals
7. The + sign indicates that there is more information that can be displayed
8. Click on the + to expand hidden information
9. The - indicates that all information is displayed
10. Click - to collapse and hide grouped information
11. Press 2 this displays Qtr 1, Qtr 2 and Grand Totals
12. Choose 3 to display all the information
13. Repeat the process for the Vertical Outline area

14. To clear the outline select Data, Ungroup, Clear Outline
15. Save the workbook as Using Outlines

Exercise 12: - Creating a Manual Outline

Manual Outline allows the user to control information that needs to be grouped together it can also be used in conjunction with the Automatic Outline.

1. Open the workbook Using Outlines
2. Select cells B1:D1

3. Choose
4. The Group dialog box appears
5. Select **C**olumns

6. Click OK
7. Repeat the process for cell F1:H1
8. The horizontal outlines are displayed above the columns headings
9. Select B1:I1, create a Manual Column Outline
10. Select A2:A5, group the rows to create a Vertical Outline
11. Save the workbook Using Outlines

Consolidation of Data

Using the Consolidation Feature allows data to be combined using independent workbooks or different worksheets.

1. Open a new workbook

2. In the worksheet create the following using formulas where applicable

	A	B	C	D	E	F
1			MS Office 2002			
2		Qtr 1	Qtr 2	Qtr 3	Qtr 4	Total
3	Word	100	200	300	400	1000
4	Excel	100	200	300	40	640
5	PowerPoint	75	75	80	125	355
6	Access	50	40	35	27	152
7	Project	25	40	50	60	175

Figure 170

3. Highlight cells A2:F7, select [Formulas] , [Define Name ▾]

4. Alternatively [Alt] [M] [M] [D] displays the New Name dialog box

5. Type the name as Table, press [OK]

6. Create a [New Folder] named Consolidation to store the workbooks

7. Save the workbook as MS Office 2002 Courses

8. Close the workbook

9. Repeat the process for MS Office 2003 and MS Office 2007

	A	B	C	D	E	F
1			MS Office 2003			
2		Qtr 1	Qtr 2	Qtr 3	Qtr 4	Total
3	Word	100	200	300	400	1000
4	Excel	100	200	300	40	640
5	PowerPoint	75	75	80	125	355
6	Access	50	40	35	27	152
7	Project	25	40	50	60	175

Figure 171

	A	B	C	D	E	F
1			MS Office 2007			
2		Qtr 1	Qtr 2	Qtr 3	Qtr 4	Total
3	Word	100	200	300	400	1000
4	Excel	100	200	300	40	640
5	PowerPoint	75	75	80	125	355
6	Access	50	40	35	27	152
7	Project	25	40	50	60	175

Figure 172

10. Ensure the workbooks MS Office 2002 Courses, 2003 and 2007 are open

11. Open a new workbook, select cell A1

12. Select Data ,

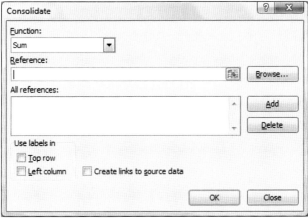

Figure 173

13. In the Function area select SUM

14. Press Browse... to locate MS Office 2002 Courses

15. Select the file, choose OK

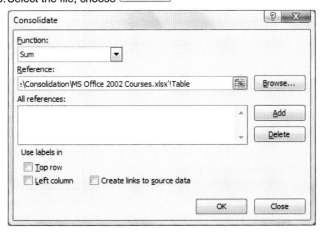

Figure 174

16. Delete the exclamation mark "!"

17. Retype !Table Consolidation\MS Office 2002 Courses.xls'!Table

18. Click [Add] to save the reference

19. Repeat steps 14 to 18 for MS Office 2003 and MS Office 2007

20. Select Use Labels, tick Top row and Left column

21. Tick Create links to source data as shown

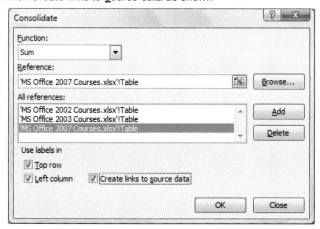

Figure 175

22. Select [OK], the consolidated worksheet appears

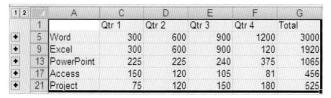

		A	C	D	E	F	G
	1		Qtr 1	Qtr 2	Qtr 3	Qtr 4	Total
+	5	Word	300	600	900	1200	3000
+	9	Excel	300	600	900	120	1920
+	13	PowerPoint	225	225	240	375	1065
+	17	Access	150	120	105	81	456
+	21	Project	75	120	150	180	525

Figure 176

23. Use the outline ⊞ and ⊟ signs to reveal or collapse the linked data

24. Save the workbook as Consolidation of Data

25. If a workbook's data is updated at any time when the consolidated worksheet is opened, the following prompt appears

Figure 177

26. Select [Options...]

Figure 178

27. Choose ◉ Enable this content

28. Click OK

Templates

A template is a means of creating a workbook that is consistent allowing such documents as Invoices, Timesheets and Balance Sheets to be used with pre set styles and formatting. When a new workbook is generated as a template it is used as the basis for the worksheet. Templates are saved to the Normal general area; however, it is possible to create a new tab for an organisation in the templates area that allows company templates to be quickly identified.

To Save a Workbook as a Template

1. Select the Office Button ,choose Save As ▸

2. Save as SMART PC Guides Timesheet

3. Click on the downward pointing arrow ▾ in the Save as type: area

4. Select Excel Template to move to the Templates area

Save as type:	Excel Template	▾

Figure 179

5. In the Template folder, click on the ⬛ New Folder icon

6. In the Name area type SMART PC Guides Template

7. Press Enter

8. Save and close the template

9. To view the template select the Office Button 🔘 , [📄 New]

10. Select [My templates...] in the template area

11. Choose the Tab [Smart PC Guides Template]

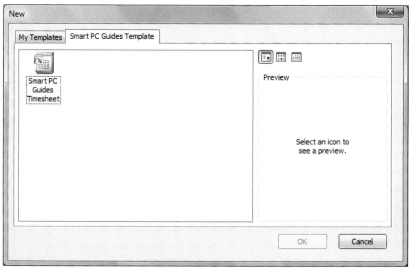

Figure 180

12. Select the SMART PC Guides Timesheet Template

13. Click [OK] to open a new workbook based on the template

Exercise 13: - Open and Amend an Existing Template

This exercise demonstrates how to customise a template quickly.

1. Click Office Button 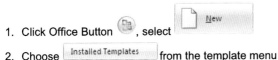, select

2. Choose Installed Templates from the template menu

3. Select Billing Statement

4. Change the font to Arial 10 with a Blue Bold font colour

5. In cell B1 replace Your Company Name with Smart PC Guides

6. In cell B4 change Zip Code to Post Code

7. In cell F12 change Zip Code to Post Code

8. In cells H15 and H16 change the currency to £ symbol

9. In cell C25 change the currency to £ symbol

10. Select Review

11. Choose Protect Sheet , click OK

12. Name the template as SMART PC Guides Billing Statement

13. Save the template in the SMART PC Guides Template area

14. Close the workbook

15. Re-open the template from the Smart PC Guides Template Tab

Using Scenario Manager

The Scenario Manager is part of the What If analysis. Each scenario added to the Scenario Manager has a defined name applied to the data. By grouping data, it is possible to use the Scenario Manager to display the outcome of what will happen to the worksheet if the data from a scenario is applied.

Creating Scenarios in a Workbook

1. Open a new workbook
2. Create the following information, insert the formulas in cells B9 and B11
3. Name the worksheet Project Expenses

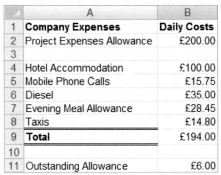

	A	B
1	**Company Expenses**	**Daily Costs**
2	Project Expenses Allowance	£200.00
3		
4	Hotel Accommodation	£100.00
5	Mobile Phone Calls	£15.75
6	Diesel	£35.00
7	Evening Meal Allowance	£28.45
8	Taxis	£14.80
9	**Total**	£194.00
10		
11	Outstanding Allowance	£6.00

Figure 181

4. Select cell B2, choose Formulas , Define Name ▾

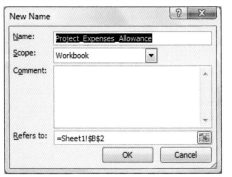

Figure 182

5. Click OK
6. Repeat steps 4 and 5 for cells B4:B9 and B11

7. Select Name Manager, the Name Manager dialog box appear

8. Alternatively [Ctrl] [F3] displays the Name Manager dialog box

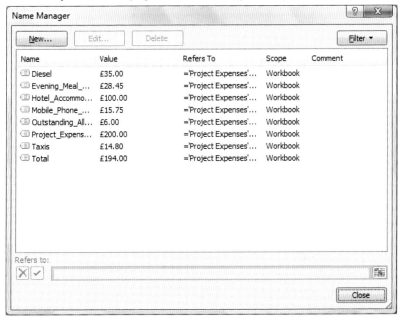

Figure 183

9. Click Close

10. Select Data , click the left  button on the arrow in What-If Analysis ▾

11. Press the option Scenario Manager

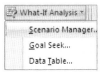

Figure 184

Figure 185

12. Press

13. Type Normal Values in the Scenario name area

14. Select the icon, highlight cells B2, B4:B8

15. Press to return to the Edit Scenario dialog box

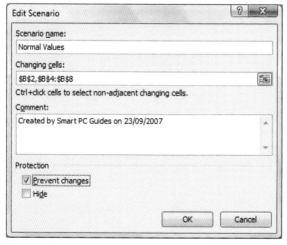

Figure 186

16. Click [OK] the Scenario Values dialog appears

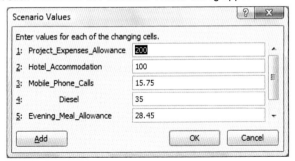

Figure 187

17. Click [OK] to return to the Scenario Manager dialog box

Figure 188

18. Repeat steps 12 to 17 to generate a Most Expensive Scenario

19. Update the values as shown on the next page

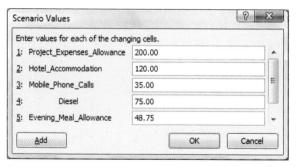

Figure 189

20. Click [OK] to display the Scenario Manager dialog box

21. Create a Least Expensive Scenario, update the values as shown below

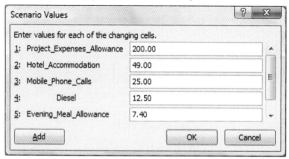

Figure 190

22. Click [OK] to display the Scenario Manager dialog box

Displaying Scenarios

1. Choose the Most Expensive Scenario, click

Figure 191

2. The data in the worksheet changes and is displayed

	A	B
1	**Company Expenses**	**Daily Costs**
2	Project Expenses Allowance	£200.00
3		
4	Hotel Accommodation	£120.00
5	Mobile Phone Calls	£35.00
6	Diesel	£75.00
7	Evening Meal Allowance	£48.75
8	Taxis	£14.80
9	**Total**	£293.55
10		
11	Outstanding Allowance	-£93.55

Figure 192

3. Repeat the process for the other scenarios

4. Re-select the Scenario Normal Values, press Show

5. To view a summary of the results select Summary...

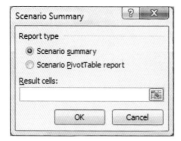

Figure 193

6. Choose Report type Scenario **s**ummary

7. Click OK

8. The Scenario Summary is displayed on a separate worksheet

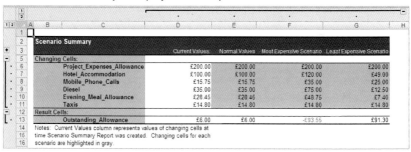

	Current Values	Normal Values	Most Expensive Scenario	Least Expensive Scenario
Scenario Summary				
Changing Cells:				
Project_Expenses_Allowance	£200.00	£200.00	£200.00	£200.00
Hotel_Accommodation	£100.00	£100.00	£120.00	£49.00
Mobile_Phone_Calls	£15.75	£15.75	£35.00	£25.00
Diesel	£35.00	£35.00	£75.00	£12.50
Evening_Meal_Allowance	£28.45	£28.45	£48.75	£7.40
Taxis	£14.80	£14.80	£14.80	£14.80
Result Cells:				
Outstanding_Allowance	£6.00	£6.00	-£93.55	£91.30

Notes: Current Values column represents values of changing cells at time Scenario Summary Report was created. Changing cells for each scenario are highlighted in gray.

Figure 194

9. Vertical and Horizontal Outlines enable data to be expanded or collapsed

10. Save the Workbook as Creating Scenarios, close the workbook

Custom Views

Custom Views enables the user to store, format and print options by selection and applies a name to a particular view.

Creating a Custom View

1. Open the workbook Creating Scenarios

2. Select the worksheet named Project Expenses

3. Highlight cells A1:B11

4. Select View , Custom Views

Figure 195

5. Click Add... , type the name as Normal Values, click OK

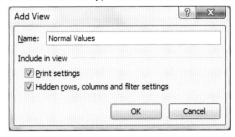

Figure 196

6. Choose the worksheet named Scenario Summary, highlight cells B2:G13

7. Select View , Custom Views , the Custom Views dialog box appears

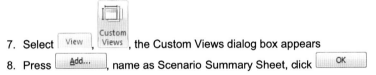

8. Press Add... , name as Scenario Summary Sheet, click OK

9. Save to update the workbook Creating Scenarios

Displaying a Custom View

1. Select  , the Custom Views dialog box appears

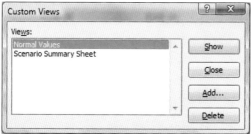

Figure 197

2. Select the view to be displayed

3. Click [Show], the defined area is displayed and highlighted

PivotTables

The PivotTable Function allows data to be viewed from a different perspective. The report appears in a table format whereby the user decides the location of the data within the workbook. The PivotTable Function automatically applies formatting to the information used. All PivotTables need to be planned to decide what information needs to be displayed.

Creating a PivotTable

1. Open up a new workbook, create the following information

	A	B	C	D	E	F
1	Name	Staff ID	Date Hired	Department	Job Title	Current Salary
2	Paul Smith	1	10/01/1965	Marketing	Marketing Administrator	£15,122
3	Jane Barrow	2	11/02/1999	Sales	Sector Director	£43,300
4	Rachael Jones	3	04/03/1990	IT	IT Helpdesk	£23,578
5	Robert Williams	4	03/02/2000	Human Resources	HR Manager	£30,500
6	James Harrow	5	22/04/1996	Marketing	Brand Manager	£27,498
7	Hannah Brown	6	10/07/1997	Marketing	Marketing Assistant	£12,750
8	Ruth Powers	7	21/02/1976	Accounts	Account Handler	£16,029

Figure 198

2. Click in the data area

3. Select [Insert], [PivotTable], [PivotTable]

4. A moving dotted line appears around the selected data

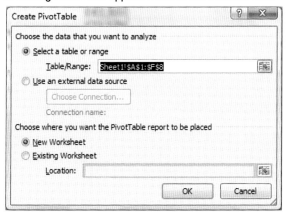

Figure 199

5. Ensure 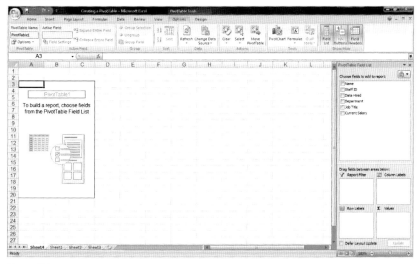 New Worksheet is selected

6. Click OK

Figure 200

7. The PivotTable Field list appears on the right hand side of the worksheet

8. From the PivotTable Field list select Name with the left 🖰 button

9. Drag the mouse pointer 🖰 to the Row Labels field box, release the mouse

10. Repeat the process moving Department to Column Labels

11. Current Salary to Values

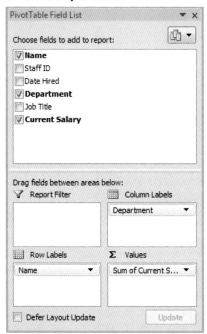

Figure 201

12. Data is automatically placed in the PivotTable on the left of the worksheet

	A	B	C	D	E	F	G
1							
2							
3	**Sum of Current Salary**	**Column Labels** ⊡					
4	**Row Labels** ⊡	**Accounts**	**Human Resources**	**IT**	**Marketing**	**Sales**	**Grand Total**
5	Hannah Brown				12750		12750
6	James Harrow				27498		27498
7	Jane Barrow					43300	43300
8	Paul Smith				15122		15122
9	Rachael Jones			23578			23578
10	Robert Williams		30500				30500
11	Ruth Powers	16029					16029
12	**Grand Total**	**16029**	**30500**	**23578**	**55370**	**43300**	**168777**

Figure 202

13. From the PivotTable Field list click the left 🖱 button on [Sum of Current Salary ▾]

14. Select [🔲 Value Field Settings...], the Value Field Settings dialog box appears

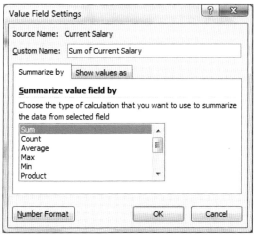

Figure 203

15. Select [Number Format], choose currency change the decimal places to zero

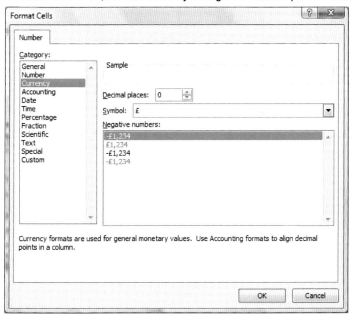

Figure 204

16. Press [OK] twice

17. The PivotTable displays the currency format

18. Save the workbook as Working with PivotTables

Changing Data in a PivotTable

1. Click on the downward arrow on the [Column Labels ▼] in the PivotTable

2. The menu expands, click with the left ⌐Ü button on [✓ (Select All)]

3. The criteria is deselected

4. Click with the left ⌐Ü button to place a tick for [✓ Marketing]

5. Press [OK]

6. The PivotTable displays the staff in Marketing

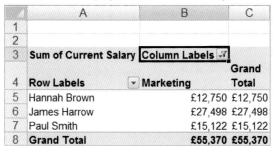

	A	B	C
1			
2			
3	**Sum of Current Salary**	**Column Labels** ▾	
4	**Row Labels** ▾	**Marketing**	**Grand Total**
5	Hannah Brown	£12,750	£12,750
6	James Harrow	£27,498	£27,498
7	Paul Smith	£15,122	£15,122
8	**Grand Total**	**£55,370**	**£55,370**

Figure 205

7. Repeat these steps to display the other departments

8. Information can be quickly restructured to display a different set of data

9. To display the data in a different format, for example staff in Marketing

10. From the PivotTable Field list click the left ⌐Ü button on [Sum of Current Salary ▼]

11. Select  , the Value Field Settings dialog box appears

Figure 206

12. Choose Count, select the ⟨Number Format⟩, select General

13. Press ⟨ OK ⟩ twice

14. The updated PivotTable displays the number of staff in Marketing

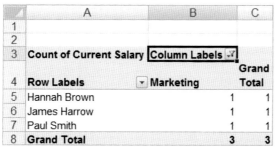

	A	B	C
1			
2			
3	**Count of Current Salary**	**Column Labels**	
4	**Row Labels**	**Marketing**	**Grand Total**
5	Hannah Brown	1	1
6	James Harrow	1	1
7	Paul Smith	1	1
8	**Grand Total**	**3**	**3**

Figure 207

15. Click on the downward arrow on the ⟨Column Labels⟩ in the PivotTable

16. Select Human Resources and IT, press ⟨ OK ⟩

17. The PivotTable is updated displaying the members of staff from Marketing, Human Resources and IT

18. From the PivotTable Field list click the left button on ⟨Count of Current Salary ▼⟩

19. Select  , the Value Field Settings dialog box appears

20. Choose Sum, press  change to currency, zero decimal places

21. Press OK twice

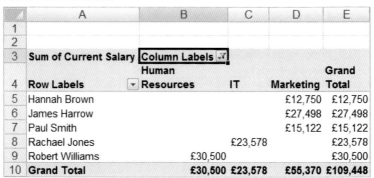

	A	B	C	D	E
1					
2					
3	**Sum of Current Salary**	**Column Labels**			
4	**Row Labels**	**Human Resources**	**IT**	**Marketing**	**Grand Total**
5	Hannah Brown			£12,750	£12,750
6	James Harrow			£27,498	£27,498
7	Paul Smith			£15,122	£15,122
8	Rachael Jones		£23,578		£23,578
9	Robert Williams	£30,500			£30,500
10	**Grand Total**	**£30,500**	**£23,578**	**£55,370**	**£109,448**

Figure 208

Naming a PivotTable

1. Ensure the Options Tab is displayed from PivotTable Tools

2. Under PivotTable Name from the PivotTable Grouping, highlight PivotTable1 and replace the text with Smart PC Guides

Figure 209

3. Press Return or Enter, save the PivotTable

Refreshing Data in a PivotTable

1. Click in the original data created in Sheet1

2. Increase Paul Smith's salary to £17,250

3. Click back in the PivotTable

4. Select Options, choose Refresh or alternatively press Alt F5

5. The PivotTable is updated

Show/Hide Field Headers

1. Click in the PivotTable data

2. Choose Options , select Field Headers , the Field Headers disappear

3. Click with the left button a second time to display the Field Headers

Show/Hide Field List

1. Click in the PivotTable data

2. Choose Options , select, Field List the Field List disappears

3. Click with the left button a second time to display the Field List

Creating a PivotChart from a PivotTable

1. Select Options from the PivotTable Tools

2. Choose PivotChart from the Tools Grouping

3. The Insert Chart dialog box appears

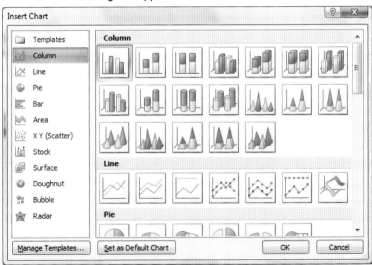

Figure 210

4. Select Clustered Cylinder, press [OK]

5. The Chart appears in the worksheet and displays the PivotTable Filter Pane

6. Double click the left 🖱 button on PivotTable Filter to move the dialog box

Adding Additional Data to a PivotChart

1. Click on the downward arrow on the [Column Labels ▼] in the PivotTable

2. Select [☑ Accounts], press [OK]

3. Data referring to Accounts appears in the PivotTable and PivotChart

4. Remove the accounts data from the PivotTable using [Column Labels ▼]

5. Save to update the workbook

Displaying a PivotChart on a Separate Sheet

1. Click anywhere in the PivotTable data

2. Press [F11], the chart appears in a separate worksheet named Chart1

3. Rename the worksheet named Chart1 to Smart PC Guides

4. Save the workbook

Customising a PivotChart

1. Click anywhere in the PivotTable data, highlight the staff in Marketing

2. Select [Options], choose Group Selection

Figure 211

3. Select the cell named Group1 the staff in Marketing

4. Rename Group1 with the name Marketing, press Return or [Enter]

	A	B	C	D	E
1					
2					
3	**Sum of Current Salary**	**Column Labels** ▼			
4	**Row Labels** ▼	**Human Resources**	**IT**	**Marketing**	**Grand Total**
5	⊟**Marketing**				
6	Hannah Brown			£12,750	£12,750
7	James Harrow			£27,498	£27,498
8	Paul Smith			£15,122	£15,122
9	⊟**Rachael Jones**				
10	Rachael Jones		£23,578		£23,578
11	⊟**Robert Williams**				
12	Robert Williams	£30,500			£30,500
13	**Grand Total**	**£30,500**	**£23,578**	**£55,370**	**£109,448**

Figure 212

5. Replace ⊟Rachael Jones with IT, press Return or Enter

6. Replace ⊟Robert Williams with Human Resources, press Return or Enter

7. Select the Sheet Tab named Smart PC Guides containing the PivotChart

8. Click anywhere in the chart, choose Design from the PivotChart Tools

9. From the Chart Layout Grouping select Layout 5

10. Change the Chart Title to Smart PC Guides

11. Change the Axis Title to Salary

12. Save the Workbook

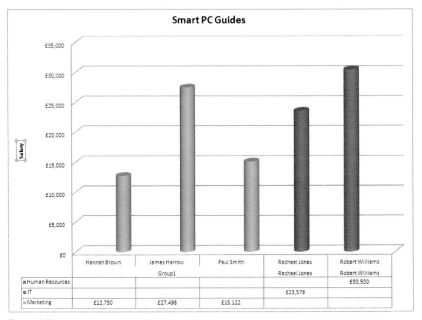

Figure 213

Macros

A Macro is a method of recording commands, keystrokes and actions that allow automated tasks.

Preparation Work before Recording a Macro

1. Write down each step of the macro

2. What should the macro do?

3. Where should the macro be stored?

4. Does the macro need to be available to other workbooks?

5. Does formatting need to be applied?

6. Does the macro need to be applied to specific cells (absolute)?

7. Does the macro need to be applied to any cells (relative)?

8. Provide an appropriate name to identify the macro

9. Do a walkthrough of the steps before recording the macro

Creating a Relative Reference Macro to Format Cells

1. Select

2. The Record Macro dialog box appears

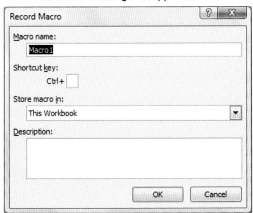

Figure 214

3. Name the macro as Formatting_Cells

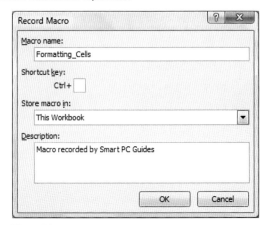

Figure 215

4. Store the macro in This Workbook

5. Use the description area to describe the Macro being created

6. Choose [OK]

7. [■] [A macro is currently recording. Click to stop recording.] appears in the Status Bar area

8. To apply relative referencing click on [View]

9. Choose [Macros ▼], [田] Use Relative References

10. The border of the icon changes to orange when use relative references is applied

11. Click in cell A1

12. Press [Ctrl] [1] to display the Format Cells dialog

13. Select the Font Tab, change the Colour to Blue

14. Select the Number Tab, set the options as shown

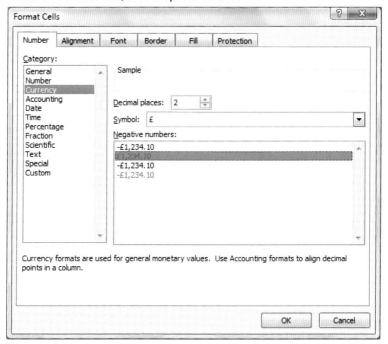

Figure 216

15. Click [OK]

16. Press [View] , [Macros] , [■ Stop Recording]

17. In cell A1, type 45, press Return or [Enter]

18. 45 has changed to £45.00 in blue font

19. Delete the information in A1, type -6, press Return, [£6.00] appears in red

20. In a series of cells type the following numbers

4	Sales A	1	2	3	4	5
5	Sales B	6	7	8	9	10
6						
7	Total	7	9	11	13	15

Figure 217

21. Select the cells containing the numbers

22. Press ⌊Alt⌋ ⌊F8⌋ to display the Macro dialog box

Figure 218

23. Choose the macro named Formatting_Cells

24. Select ⌊Run⌋

25. The numbers are formatted automatically using the macro

Deleting a Macro

1. Select ⌊Alt⌋ ⌊F8⌋

2. Choose the macro to be deleted, select ⌊Delete⌋

3. The following dialog box appears

Figure 219

4. Choose ⌊Yes⌋, the macro is deleted

Note: If the Macro has been saved in the PERSONAL.XLSB area you will need to unhide the workbook using the unhide command found under the View command.

Exercise 14: - Creating a Header and Footer Macro

1. Create a macro and name it Header_Footer

2. Store the macro in Personal Macro Workbook

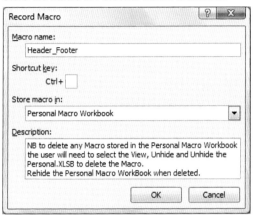

3. Type and centre a heading named **Smart PC Guides**

4. In the bottom left Footer area type V1.0

5. In the Centre Footer area type Page &[Page] of &[Pages]

6. In the bottom right Footer area choose 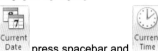 press spacebar and

7. Click Stop Recording

8. Click on a new workbook

9. In cell A1 type =Today() to insert the date

10. Select View, Macros, View Macros

11. Run the macro named Header_Footer

12. Preview the results

Create a Relative Macro for a Web Address

To create a macro to produce a company Web address, widen the column to display the address in the cell and the macro stored in the Personal.xls Macro Workbook. When the Macro is stored in the Personal macro workbook, it can used with any workbook.

1. Select  , Record Macro...

2. The Record Macro dialog box appears

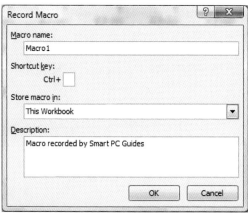

Figure 220

3. Name the macro as Web_Address

4. Store the macro in This Workbook

5. Choose

6. ◻ A macro is currently recording. Click to stop recording. appears in the Status Bar area

7. Select View , Macros ▾

8. Ensure a orange border is around ⊞ Use Relative References to show it is activated

9. Select cell A1, press Ctrl K

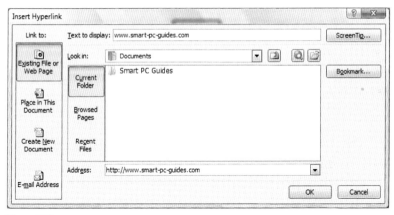

Figure 221

10. Complete the **T**ext to display and Addr**e**ss boxes, press [OK]

11. Widen the column to fit the web address in the cell

12. Select [View], [Macros], [Stop Recording]

13. Press [View], [Macros], [View Macros] or press [Alt] [F8]

14. Select All Open Workbooks

Figure 222

15. Select **PERSONAL.XLSB!Web_Address**

16. Press  to view the results of the macro

Quick Access Toolbar

The Quick Access Toolbar keeps commands that are frequently used. The items are readily available regardless of which of the Ribbon's Tabs a user is working in. The Quick Access Toolbar is located above the ribbon (default)

Figure 223

or below The Ribbon.

Figure 224

Displaying the Quick Access Toolbar below the Ribbon

1. Click with the left 🖱 button on the downward pointing arrow ⬇ to open the Customise Quick Access Toolbar menu

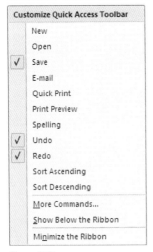

Figure 225

2. Click with the left 🖱 button on │ Print Preview │

3. The Print Preview Icon 🔍 is displayed on the toolbar

4. Click with the left 🖱 button on the downward pointing arrow ⏷

5. Select More Commands...

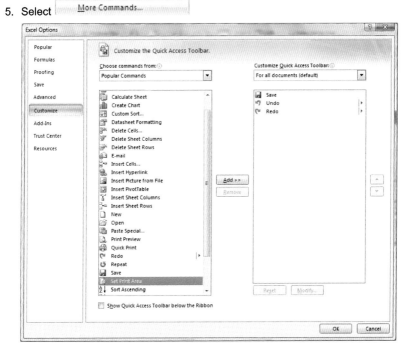

Figure 226

6. From the Popular Commands select Set Print Area, press Add >>

7. The feature is now displayed in the Quick Access Toolbar area

8. Reposition items using the ▲ and ▼ arrows

9. Click Popular Commands ▼ , the menu is expanded

10. Click OK

Remove a Command from the Quick Access Toolbar

1. Press with the right 🖱 button over the command to be removed

2. Click Remove from Quick Access Toolbar

3. The command is removed from the Quick Access Toolbar

Excel File Formats

Excel 2007 uses file formats that are different from those used in previous versions of Excel. By not using the new formats some of the new features of Excel 2007 may be lost.

Formats used in Excel 2007

Excel Workbook: The new binary workbook format that enables the new features of Excel 2007 also speeds up your work. Files saved in this format cannot be opened in earlier versions of Excel unless the translating filter programme has been downloaded. The new binary workbook format will be seen with an added x, for example **.xlsx**

Excel Macro-Enabled Workbook: This format is the same as the Workbook format with the addition of macros. The format will be saved as **.xlsm**

XML Spreadsheet: The XML document format is a plain text file that includes all the text and XML coding and has proved to be the most popular technology for exchanging data regardless of the hardware platform or operating system being used. This format will be saved as **.xml**

Excel Template: A new form of template in Excel 2007 that enables the new features of the programme. The new format will be saved with an added x, for example **.xltx**

Excel Macro-Enables Template: This format is the same as the Excel Template with the addition of macros. The new format will be saved with an added x, for example **.xltxm**

Excel 97-2003 Format: The binary format used in previous versions of Excel. Using this format disables some of the new features of Excel 2007. This format will be saved as **.xls**

Excel 97-2003 Format Template: The binary file format for templates used in previous versions of Excel. This format will be saved as **.xlt**

Single File Web Page: This format is used to create a web page and stores the graphics in the same file.

Web Page: Creates a standard HTML-format web page where graphics are stored on a separate file. This format will be saved as **.htm**

Rich Text Format: This binary file contains text and formatting. This format will be saved as **.rtf**

Plain Text: This file format contains just the text of the document and no formatting. This format will be saved as **.txt**

Notes Pages

Shortcut Keys

SHORTCUT KEYS	DESCRIPTION	SHORTCUT KEYS	DESCRIPTION
Ctrl F1	Hide or Display the Ribbon	Ctrl Shift P	Format Cells Dialog Box
Ctrl Shift $	Currency 2 Decimal Places	Ctrl F2	Displays Print Preview
Ctrl Shift !	Number 2 Decimal Places	Shift F3	Insert Function Dialog Box
Ctrl Shift +	Insert Cells, Rows, Columns	F1	Excel Help
Ctrl -	Delete Cells, Rows, Columns	F2	Edit Active Cell
Ctrl 1	Format Cells	F5	Displays Go To Dialog Box
Ctrl 2	Apply or Remove Bold Format	F7	Spell Checker
Ctrl 3	Apply or Remove Italic Format	F10	Displays Shortcut Keys
Ctrl 4	Apply or Remove Underlining	F11	Creates a Chart
Ctrl 5	Apply or Remove Strikethrough	F12	Save As Dialog Box
Ctrl B	Apply or Remove Bold Format	Alt P F	Print Dialog Box
Ctrl C	Copy Cells	Alt P W	Page Layout View
Ctrl P	Displays Print Dialog Box	Ctrl F3	Displays Name Manager
Ctrl S	Saves the Workbook	Alt W M	Watch Window Dialog Box
Ctrl U	Apply or Remove Underline	Alt D M	Trace Dependents
Ctrl V	Paste Cells	Alt P M	Trace Precedents
Ctrl X	Cuts Information	Alt F8	Displays Macro Dialog Box
Ctrl Y	Repeats Previous Command		
Ctrl Z	Undo Previous Command		

This concludes the Excel 2007 Foundation to Expert Guide. Thank you for choosing Smart PC Guides. Please visit our website www.smart-pc-guides.com to view our complete range of Smart PC Guides.

Index